This book is dedicated to Mrs. Odessa Beaty and Mr. .... Owens,

the caring adults who gave us a lifetime of wisdom, strength and courage.

We thank them all for having been in our lives for this reason, season and lifetime.

"People come into your life for a reason, a season or a lifetime.

When you figure out which it is, you know exactly what to do."

Michelle Ventor

HEROES

David Lewis   Bobby Garrett

Neil Shorthouse   Reid Carpenter

"Get young people turned on to living, so we can get them turned on to learning."

Bill Milliken

FOUNDATION FOR EDUCATIONAL SUCCESS

207 Bank Station, PMB #660
Fayetteville, Georgia 30215
770-716-9238
www.theffes.com

ONLINE CURRICULUM VERSION AVAILABLE

AUTHORS' WORDS

As we travel throughout the country conducting our workshops and presentations, we ask youth this question: "What do you want to be when you grow up?" All too often this question is answered by a shrug of the shoulders, indicating they have no idea what they want to do with their lives. When we do get a verbal response, it is mostly the canned answers of doctor, lawyer, professional athlete, or another occupation that is not well thought out. These are the sorts of responses that youth think we, as adults, want to hear.

Our inspiration for writing this book is simple - we want to make a difference in the lives of youth by empowering them with what they need to be successful. We want to help them begin to figure out who they are, what it is that they want to do with their lives, and how to go about doing it. This book, *Faces of Change 2*, will help youth take a serious inventory of their lives and help them begin to plan for successful futures by developing their talents, interests, and abilities.

Most adults want to help kids grow and become successful, but many don't have the necessary skills to do so. This book will help guide adults through the process of helping youth grow and will provide ways to help youth clearly define their goals. Adults can help youth discover their purpose and give them direction through deliberate, intentional connections and interactions with them.

We believe that two of the greatest days in a person's life are the day you were born and the day you discover why you were born. Many young people today are not discovering their purpose until late in life after much trial and error. *Faces of Change 2* will empower youth to take ownership of their lives and give them a plan for accomplishing their goals and achieving their dreams.

In our decades of working as advocates for youth, we know young people don't care how much you know until they know how much you care. This book provides adults with a process that helps young people realize how much adults care. *Faces of Change 2* gives youth and adults an opportunity to work together to build a great future.

Reginald B. Beaty
Tony L. Owens

GETTING STARTED

Caring Adult,

Congratulations! As a parent, grandparent, godparent, coach, mentor, or other caring adult, you have taken an important step to ensure that the young person in your life is a success by purchasing this book. As you work through each lesson with the young person or persons who are the recipients of this gift, you will probably experience a change in the way that you feel about success. You will not only be supporting young people, but this book will also have a positive impact on you regardless of your age.

Young Person,

Congratulations! Someone in your life cares about your success. They have not only acquired this valuable resource, but in securing this book they have also pledged to work with you as you systematically develop skills that you will need to be successful. These are the skills that you will need not only as a student, but in all endeavors of your life. If your dream is to be an award-winning entertainer, a world class athlete or the next president of the United States you will need to plan deliberately. This book, along with the support from a caring adult in your life, provides you with the roadmap you will need on your path to success. The information in the book is directed towards you.

How to Use This Book

All of the activities are designed for you to read and to discuss with a caring adult. In many of the units both of you will be asked to complete an activity and then discuss your responses. These are opportunities for quality dialogue to support you in acquiring the identified skills. Each unit consists of a short **OVERVIEW** that tells you what the unit is about. Following the overview, you will see the **NONCOGNITIVE VARIABLE(S)** the unit addresses. Following the noncognitive variable(s), is the **LESSON** for each unit presented in an interesting manner. After the lesson, you are provided **FOOD FOR THOUGHT** in the form of an inspirational quote and/or poem which provides you with an opportunity to think deeper about the lesson. The **WHAT YOU SHOULD KNOW** section provides you with the central ideas that you should understand after engaging in the lesson. Finally, the unit ends with an **ACTIVITY** that allows you to apply your new-found knowledge. Each of these areas provides rich opportunities for you to have a conversation with your caring adult about your thoughts and ideas. After completing all of the lessons you will have developed a roadmap to achieve the goals that will lead to your success.

Enjoy your journey!

WHY AND HOW TO GET YOUTH READY FOR LIFE!

Faces of Change 2 provides a framework to assist and empower you with skills and disciplines that will prepare you for a lifetime of success. This book is a wonderful resource to help prepare you for a bright future. Each unit is filled with nuggets of information that will provoke you to use critical thinking when confronting obstacles in life that could possibly prevent you from reaching your dreams!

Have you ever been asked, "What do you want to be when you grow up?" In response, you may have shrugged your shoulders, indicating that you have no idea; or you offered the typical response of what adults want to hear. Become a doctor, lawyer, nurse or professional athlete. Of course, there's nothing wrong with any of those responses, but is it what you want to do?

Should life afford you the privilege of time, inevitably you will become an adult. What is not inevitable is you will become a well-equipped adult who is ready to successfully meet and conquer the challenges of adulthood. You must carefully plan it.

There are countless books that help plan for life. However, *Faces of Change 2* is different because it provides a roadmap for you to strategically chart your course for achieving success. Each unit provides relevant real-world situations with practical methods for addressing them. You are guided to use the unlimited power within you to become a person ready and prepared to take your rightful place in this world.

Adults make assumptions regarding the needs of youth. Some of these assumptions have left a portion of youth without the proper instructions to be prepared for life. Listed below are some assumptions adults often make:

- The older youth are, the less they need adult help.
- As young people get older, they automatically become wiser.
- Youth mature mentally and physically at the same rate.
- Youth do not listen.
- Youth really do not need adult help.
- Some things should be common sense.
- If it makes sense to adults, it should make sense to youth.
- Youth today do not act like they need adult help.
- Most youth have the same experiences/opportunities.

TABLE OF CONTENTS

NONCOGNITIVE VARIABLES (NCVs)

Faces of Change 2 incorporates over thirty years of proven research by Dr. William Sedlacek regarding the positive impact on a young person's life after acquiring the eight noncognitive skills. *Faces of Change 2* is specifically designed to facilitate the deliberate acquisition of noncognitive variables.

What are Noncognitive Variables?

Noncognitive Variables (NCVs) are those attributes that speak to adjustments, motivations and perceptions. There is a great deal of evidence that noncoginitive variables can be a great predictor of academic success, retention, and graduation for both traditional and non-traditional students.

Facts About Noncognitive Variables:

- In the Gates Millennium Scholars program, a review of an entire application is scored on the noncognitive variables, and makes up 80% of the weight used in selection.

- 11,000 Gates Scholars have attended more than 1,450 different colleges and universities with a 97% first-year retention rate, an 87% five-year retention rate and a 78% five-year graduation rate.

- Teachers, advisors, or counselors who use the system can expect to obtain better student outcomes in terms of grades and retention, as well as greater satisfaction themselves in employing something systematic with demonstrated utility in an area that often produces confusion and anxiety.

- Oregon State University (OSU) noncognitive scores correlate with retention; and since employing noncognitive variables, the OSU retention rate is higher

Students who have done well in school tend to have a person of strong influence who provides advice to them particularly in times of crisis and encouragement. This variable involves having someone beyond a role model, although that may be part of the relationship. A strong support person takes an active role in advising and directing someone.

"I see publication after publication designed to help students that are either too theoretical to assist most users or that ignore research and are unprofessional. Beaty and Owens have taken the eight noncognitive variables that I and others have studied over the years and designed some useful assessments and examples that demonstrate how one can work with each variable to achieve academic and life success. In their instructional guide, Beaty and Owens manage to accomplish what most authors cannot: Good practical advice based on research and theory."

Dr. William Sedlacek, Author - Beyond the Big Test
Professor Emeritus the University of Maryland, College Park

NONCOGNITIVE VARIABLES (NCVs)

POSITIVE SELF-CONCEPT

- Demonstrates confidence, strength of character, determination, and independence.

DEMONSTRATED COMMUNITY SERVICE

- Identifies with a community, is involved in community work.

AVAILABILITY OF STRONG SUPPORT PERSON

- Seeks and takes advantage of a strong support network or has someone to turn to in a crisis or for encouragement.

SUCCESSFUL LEADERSHIP EXPERIENCE

- Demonstrates strong leadership in any area: church, sports, non-educational groups, gang leader, etc.

PREFERS LONG-RANGE TO SHORT-TERM OR IMMEDIATE NEEDS

- Able to respond to deferred gratification; plans ahead and sets goals.

NONTRADITIONAL KNOWLEDGE ACQUIRED

- Acquires knowledge in a sustained and/or culturally related ways in any area, including social, personal, or interpersonal.

UNDERSTANDS AND KNOWS HOW TO HANDLE THE SYSTEM

- Exhibits a realistic view of the system based upon personal experiences and is committed to improving the existing system. Takes an assertive approach to dealing with existing wrongs, but is not hostile to society nor is a "cop-out." Involves handling any "isms" (e.g., racism, sexism).

REALISTIC SELF-APPRAISAL

- Recognizes and accepts any strengths and deficiencies, especially academic, and works hard at self-development. Recognizes need to broaden individuality.

SACRIFICE/COMMITMENT – CHICKEN AND PIG

In this unit, you will explore the difference between making a sacrifice versus making a commitment. You will learn that making a sacrifice and making a commitment are clearly two different things. There are several key people that must be involved as you go through the *Faces of Change 2* process. First, there is you, the person who must totally commit to the process and also several caring adults who will sacrifice a part of themselves to help you navigate through this process.

NONCOGNITIVE VARIABLE(S)

- **REALISTIC SELF-APPRAISAL:** Recognizes and accepts any strengths and deficiencies, especially academic, and works hard at self-development. Recognizes need to broaden individuality.

LESSON

SACRIFICE	**COMMITMENT**

"Let us sacrifice our today so that our children can have a better tomorrow."

A. P. J. Abdul Kalam

"People who put themselves on the line and sacrifice their own safety for the greater good and for others, and anyone in any profession whose concern is the welfare for other people instead of the individual, are inspiring and important."

Chris Hemsworth

SHORT-TERM - short period of time.

"Unless commitment is made, there are only promises and hopes... but no plans."

Peter Drucker

"Desire is the key to motivation, but it's determination and commitment to an unrelenting pursuit of your goal – a commitment to excellence – that will enable you to attain the success you seek."

Mario Andretti

LONG-TERM - long period of time.

When you say that you will make a sacrifice to a purpose, that means you are willing to give up something to make time to fulfill that purpose. The sacrifices you make will determine whether or not that purpose is fulfilled. Your adult guide will be the person who is willing to sacrifice their time, energy, talent, and wisdom to help you through this process.

When you are committed to something that means you are willing to give up everything until that something becomes a reality. The essence of every major goal you accomplish in life will be determined by your desire to want it so bad you are willing to commit to it. You are the primary planner in this process, which means you must commit to it.

FOOD FOR THOUGHT

Be the Best of Whatever You Are

If you can't be a pine on the top of the hill
Be a scrub in the valley—but be
The best little scrub by the side of the rill;
Be a bush if you can't be a tree.
If you can't be a bush be a bit of the grass,
And some highway some happier make;
If you can't be a muskie then just be a bass—
But the liveliest bass in the lake!
We can't all be captains, we've got to be crew,
There's something for all of us here.
There's big work to do and there's lesser to do,
And the task we must do is the near.
If you can't be a highway then just be a trail,
If you can't be the sun be a star;
It isn't by size that you win or you fail—
Be the best of whatever you are!

Douglas Malloch

WHAT YOU SHOULD KNOW

Definition of sacrifice

Definition of commitment

Difference between making a sacrifice and a commitment

ACTIVITY: SACRIFICE/COMMITMENT – CHICKEN AND PIG

Name:	Date:

One day a chicken and a pig were walking through the forest. The chicken said, "I have an excellent idea that I want to share with you, pig." The pig asked, "What is this great idea?" The chicken proceeded to tell the pig that he felt they needed to give back to society and they should both go down to the nearest homeless shelter and provide breakfast to the residents. As they continued their walk, the chicken told the pig that they could both contribute to the breakfast. The pig stopped. Being a little puzzled, the pig wanted some clarity on exactly what they would be serving to everyone at the breakfast. The chicken responded, "Why just a very simple breakfast of bacon, eggs and toast." The pig thought for a moment and then said, "It may be a simple breakfast for you because you will just be sacrificing a few eggs. I will have to commit my life in order to give some bacon to this breakfast." Though both acts are great and noble, both require different levels of participation.

SACRIFICE
How would you define **sacrifice**?
Why is the chicken's contribution considered a sacrifice?

COMMITMENT
How would you define **commitment**?
Why is the pig's contribution considered a commitment?

Identify two or three short-term academic goals and two or three long-term academic goals. After identifying your goals, write the type of commitment required to reach the goal.

Short-Term Academic Goals	Short-Term Commitments
1.	1.
2.	2.
3.	3.
Long-Term Academic Goals	Long-Term Commitments
1.	1.
2.	2.
3.	3.

With your life being a parable of the breakfast, refer back to the last three sentences in the story about the chicken and pig. Though both acts are great and noble, both require different levels of participation.

What level of participation would be required of you when it comes to planning your life, sacrifice or commitment? Why?
Response:
What level of participation would be required of your caring adult and others when it comes to planning your life, sacrifice or commitment? Why?
Response:

Essay

Choose an event in history during which someone made a great **sacrifice** or select your own (example: historical event or a war). Describe what the sacrifice was and why it was worth making the sacrifice.

Choose an event in history during which someone made a great **commitment** or select your own (example: historical event or a war). Describe what the commitment was and why it was worth making the commitment.

ATTITUDE

In this unit, you will be introduced to an important characteristic in life: ATTITUDE. Having the proper attitude and outlook in life is essential to achieving success. Committing to the *Faces of Change 2* process will help you set and achieve goals, which leads to a can-do ATTITUDE while working to achieve success.

NONCOGNITIVE VARIABLE(S)

- **REALISTIC SELF-APPRAISAL:** Recognizes and accepts any strengths and deficiencies, especially academic, and works hard at self-development. Recognizes need to broaden individuality.

LESSON

Attitude can be defined as one's general disposition, one's natural mental and emotional outlook or mood: it is our predominant state of mind. Attitude is the key factor that most determines how one reacts to the circumstances of life, and how well one can handle life's circumstances to continue towards one's goals.

"It is your ATTITUDE, not your aptitude, that will determine your altitude."

FOOD FOR THOUGHT

Attitude

The longer I live, the more I realize the impact of attitude on life.

It is more important than the past, than education, than money, than circumstances,

than failures, than successes, than what other people think or say or do.

It is more important than appearance, giftedness or skill.

It will make or break a company, a church or a home.

The remarkable thing is we have a choice every day regarding

the attitude we will embrace for that day,

We cannot change the inevitable.

The only thing we can do is play on the one string we have, and that is our ATTITUDE!

I am convinced that life is 10% what happens to me and 90% how I react to it.

And so it is with you . . . we are in charge of our ATTITUDE.

Charles Swindoll

WHAT YOU SHOULD KNOW

Definition of attitude

How and/or why attitude affects life

Why it is important to give 100% in all you do

ACTIVITY: ATTITUDE

Name:	Date:

What does ATTITUDE really equal?

Complete the exercise below to see how this adds up.

Step 1 - Insert numerical placement of each letter in the word "**ATTITUDE**" on line 2 of table 1 below each letter on line 1 as it appears in table 2.

Step 2 - Add the numbers on line 2 and place sum in last box below total box with the percentage sign.

Table 1

LINE 1	A	T	T	I	T	U	D	E	TOTAL
LINE 2									%

Table 2

A	B	C	D	E	F	G	H	I	J	K	L	M
1	2	3	4	5	6	7	8	9	10	11	12	13

N	O	P	Q	R	S	T	U	V	W	X	Y	Z
14	15	16	17	18	19	20	21	22	23	24	25	26

In the exercise above what does Attitude equal?

2. In the ATTITUDE passage by Swindoll, why do you think he believes that attitude is more important than the things he listed in the parable (past, education, money, circumstances, failures, successes, appearance, giftedness, skill, what other people think, say or do)?

3. What does Swindoll mean when he says attitude can make or break a company, church, or home?

4. Do you believe that every day you make a choice regarding the attitude you will embrace?

5. Give examples of situations in which you make a choice regarding your attitude.

6. What one string was Mr. Swindoll referring to in the passage on the previous page?

INTRODUCTION TO FACES OF CHANGE 2 – TIMELINE

This unit will give an initial orientation to the Timeline. The first step of planning your future is to write your plan down. Planning and preparing for success requires writing it down. Writing your plans down provides a visual reference when needed. It is much easier to keep moving toward your goals when you have them clearly in sight. Additionally, it is much easier to get sidetracked and possibly delayed, or even completely derailed from reaching your goals without written plans.

Faces of Change 2 Timeline is the tool you will use to prepare a well-defined visual plan for your success. The Timeline will serve as a template to help you develop a written plan that specifically outlines where you are going and what you will achieve in life. This unit will give an initial orientation to the Timeline.

ALL NONCOGNITIVE VARIABLES

LESSON

There are three moments in time you must consider as you go through this process and develop your plan for life. First, let's take a look as they are presented on the *Faces of Change 2* Timeline. Looking at the middle of your *Faces of Change 2* Timeline, you will see the words, **PAST, PRESENT** and **FUTURE.** These three words and what they represent encompass your whole life.

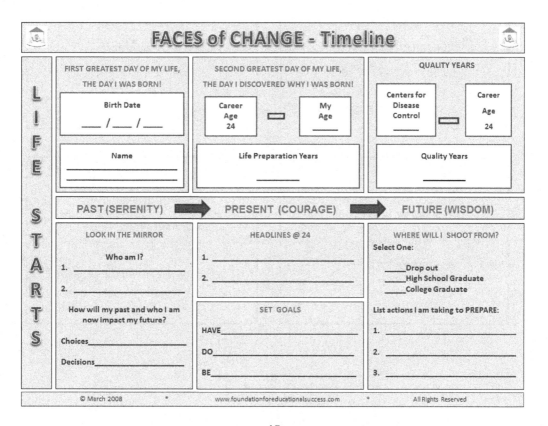

You will notice in parenthesis the words **SERENITY, COURAGE,** and **WISDOM.** These words represent the state of mind or position you must assume during the corresponding period of your life. Take a look at the diagram below to get a clearer understanding of all six words.

PAST	**PRESENT**	**FUTURE**
existed or taking place in a period before the present	period of time occurring now	at a later time; going or likely to happen
SERENITY	**COURAGE**	**WISDOM**
the state of being calm, peaceful, and untroubled	the ability to do something that frightens you	the quality of having experience, knowledge, and good judgment

To put the past behind you,
you must accept that
you've moved beyond it.

The longer you live in the past,
the less future
you have to enjoy.

No matter how dirty
your past is,
your future is spotless.

*"Yesterday's the past,
tomorrow's the future,
but today is a gift.
That's why it's called the present."*

Bil Keane

FOOD FOR THOUGHT

Here Comes the Future

Imagine you were looking into a crystal ball and you could see your future. Stare down the road, across fields, down rivers, over mountains and across oceans and see all of the positive experiences that await you. Dream of all of the possibilities that are available to you.

As you look into your crystal ball it becomes clearer and more focused and you see all of the possibilities. Look around to see what are those factors that contribute to the positive activities on your journey. You have an optimistic future ahead of you. The future realizes that your ultimate goals must be central to your purpose in life.

This view shows you what you will achieve, where you will go and what things you will accomplish. What will history write about you? Continue to look into the crystal ball. You see the story of your future and the opportunities that are in store for you. It is your time to live life to its fullest and to have the kind of life that you want.

Your future starts at this moment. You have been given the gift of insight into the future. Do not squander any of your resources. Treat every moment with care. The future is for you to design yourself, whatever you want to be.

Anonymous

WHAT YOU SHOULD KNOW

Purpose of *Faces of Change 2* Timeline

Reasonable knowledge of the three words PAST, PRESENT, FUTURE

Reasonable knowledge of the three words SERENITY, COURAGE, WISDOM

ACTIVITY: INTRODUCTION TO FACES OF CHANGE 2 – TIMELINE

Name:	Date:

Read the passages below, choose your favorite, then in your own words describe what that passage means to you.

Passage 1

How did it get so late so soon? Its night before its afternoon. December is here before its June. My goodness how the time has flewn. How did it get so late so soon?

Dr. Seuss

Response:

Passage 2

Grant me the SERENITY (Past) to accept the things I cannot change,
COURAGE (Present) to change the things I can,
and WISDOM (Future) to know the difference.

Response:

Passage 3

Don't cry over the past, it's gone.
Don't stress about the future, it hasn't arrived.
Live in the present and make it beautiful.

Response:

FACES of CHANGE - Timeline

L I F E   **S T A R T S**

PAST (SERENITY)

FIRST GREATEST DAY OF MY LIFE,
THE DAY I WAS BORN!

Birth Date

___ / ___ / ___

Name

_____

LOOK IN THE MIRROR

Who am I?

1. _____
2. _____

How will my past and who I am now impact my future?

Choices _____

Decisions _____

PRESENT (COURAGE)

SECOND GREATEST DAY OF MY LIFE,
THE DAY I DISCOVERED WHY I WAS BORN!

| Career Age 24 | | My Age ___ |

Life Preparation Years

HEADLINES @ 24

1. _____
2. _____

SET GOALS

HAVE _____

DO _____

BE _____

FUTURE (WISDOM)

QUALITY YEARS

| Centers for Disease Control ___ | | Career Age 24 |

Quality Years

WHERE WILL I SHOOT FROM?

Select One:

___ Drop out
___ High School Graduate
___ College Graduate

List actions I am taking to PREPARE:

1. _____
2. _____
3. _____

© March 2008   www.foundationforeducationalsuccess.com   * All Rights Reserved

1.0 THE GREAT DIVIDE – WARM UP, HEROES

In this unit, you, along with your caring adult, will take a look at the worlds in which you each live. While at times you may feel as if your world is very different than that of the adults around you, the truth is that they aren't. Both worlds share common ground, and your world will eventually become the same as an adult. Through completing and sharing assessments you, along with your adult guides, will gain a better picture of both worlds so that you can begin to figure out who you eventually want to be.

NONCOGNITIVE VARIABLE(S)

- **AVAILABILITY OF STRONG SUPPORT PERSON:** Seeks and takes advantage of a strong support network or has someone to turn to in a crisis or for encouragement.

LESSON

"When you are through
changing, you are through."

Bruce Barton

"Life is a series of collisions with the future;
it is not the sum of what we have been,
but what we yearn to be."

Jose Ortega y Gasset

From a young age, all of us form an idea of what a hero is and what he/she does. We admire these heroes, look up to them and, knowingly or unknowingly, pattern our lives after them. All of us need heroes who are willing to help us as we journey through life. These heroes may be big or small, known throughout the world or just hold a special place in our heart.

FOOD FOR THOUGHT

Heroes

Everyday somewhere in the world another unsung hero is born.

Someone who is willing, to lay his life on the line

to save another living creature, on this wonderful planet of ours.

To go out of their way, and risk life and limb to save something, from danger and certain death.

These unsung heroes don't want medals, glory or even fame.

In fact, most would walk away afterwards, without anyone ever knowing their name.

It is not that they feel guilty.

They just feel that they haven't done anything that is special

or something someone else wouldn't have probably done.

Therefore, to all those unsung heroes this poem is just for you.

For all the lives that you save each and every day.

David Harris

WHAT YOU SHOULD KNOW

The importance of continuously growing and improving your life

The heroes in your life who can assist you as you grow

How your personal heroes have impacted your life

ACTIVITY: 1.0 THE GREAT DIVIDE – WARM UP, HEROES

Name:	Date:

Below in the column on the left labeled "HEROES" name some important or influential adults in your life. In the column on the right labeled "IMPACT" explain the impact they made in your life. Remember to keep these people in mind as you complete the *Faces of Change 2* lessons.

Heroes	Impact on Your World
1.	1.
2.	2.
3.	3.
4.	4.
5.	5.

Select three or four people you named in the list above then identify a way you want to thank them for how they have impacted your life thus far (via: card, phone call, note, email, text message, etc.).

Caring Adult	Act of Appreciation
1.	1.
2.	2.
3.	3.
4.	4.

Most of the people you listed as heroes are willing to serve as a strong support person who will have a word of advice and encouragement as you move forward. This is also an excellent time to ask one or two of them to serve as one of the caring adults you would like to call on as you complete the *Faces of Change 2* process.

1.1 YOUR WORLD

In this unit, you will observe and record the immediate cares, thoughts, concerns and behaviors that fill your world. This information will be used to compare and contrast your world with that of adults. Your world and that of adults sometimes seem distant and far apart, each world having its own cares, concerns, and patterns of thought, making the two worlds appear to be separated by a great divide. The reality is that your world and that of an adult are not far apart at all.

NONCOGNITIVE VARIABLE(S)

- **AVAILABILITY OF STRONG SUPPORT PERSON:** Seeks and takes advantage of a strong support network or has someone to turn to in a crisis or for encouragement.

- **REALISTIC SELF-APPRAISAL:** Recognizes and accepts any strengths and deficiencies, especially academic, and works hard at self-development. Recognizes need to broaden individuality.

LESSON

How many times have you heard an adult say something like, "I don't know what's wrong with kids today; they just don't seem to get it." How many times have you said something like, "Adults just don't understand; they don't know what it's like to be a kid." Maybe there is some truth in both of these statements. The world of adults and your world can at times seem to be very different, which creates this GREAT DIVIDE between the two of you.

You will need adults to help you grow and mature into a capable, prepared adult. In this unit, you will work with your caring adult(s) to build a firm foundation and reach across the perceived great divide that separates you from them. Upon this foundation, you and your caring adult will move towards developing some of the skills you will need to transition into adulthood.

"Those who improve with age embrace the power of personal growth and personal achievement and begin to replace youth with wisdom, innocence with understanding, and lack of purpose with self-actualization."

Bo Bennett

FOOD FOR THOUGHT

Don't Quit

When things go wrong as they sometimes will,

When the road you're trudging seems all uphill,

When funds are low and the debts are high,

And you want to smile, but you have to sigh.

When care is pressing you down a bit.

Rest, if you must, but don't you quit.

Life is queer with its twists and turns,

As every one of us sometimes learns.

And many a failure turns about.

When he might have won had he stuck it out:

Don't give up though the pace seems slow –

You may succeed with another blow.

Success is failure turned inside out –

The silver tint of the clouds of doubt.

And you never can tell how close you are.

It may be near when it seems so far:

So, stick to the fight when you are hardest hit.

It's when things seem worst that you must not quit.

Anonymous

WHAT YOU SHOULD KNOW

Cares, thoughts, concerns and behaviors that characterize your world

Cares, thoughts, concerns and behaviors that characterize adults in your world

Those things that youth and adults have in common

ACTIVITY: 1.1 YOUR WORLD

Name:	Date:

As a young person growing up in today's world, how do you see things? Help give the caring adult who will be working with you a glimpse inside your world. In the space below list as many of the cares, thoughts, concerns, and behaviors which come to mind that are important to you. List those things that fill your world and the lives of people in your world. Be open and honest. (e.g. fitting in, clothes...)

Responses	
1.	2.
3.	4.
5.	6.
7.	8.
9.	10.
11.	12.
13.	14.
15.	16.
17.	18.
19.	20.
21.	22.
23.	24.
25.	26.
27.	28.
29.	30.
31.	32.

1.2 ADULT WORLD

In this unit, you will work with your caring adult(s) to build a firm foundation by reaching across the great divide that separates you from them. As you begin building a foundation, you will work to develop skills needed during transition into adulthood. As previously mentioned, your world and that of adults sometimes seem distant and far apart, each world having its own cares, concerns, and patterns of thought. While the worlds may at times seem separated by a great divide, the reality is that your world and adults are not far apart at all and working together brings greater success.

NONCOGNITIVE VARIABLE(S)

- **AVAILABILITY OF STRONG SUPPORT PERSON:** Seeks and takes advantage of a strong support network or has someone to turn to in a crisis or for encouragement.

- **REALISTIC SELF-APPRAISAL:** Recognizes and accepts any strengths and deficiencies, especially academic, and works hard at self-development. Recognizes need to broaden individuality.

LESSON

You will need adults to help you grow and mature into capable and prepared adults. Observe and record the immediate cares, thoughts, concerns and behaviors that fill your world. This information will be used to compare and contrast your world with that of adults.

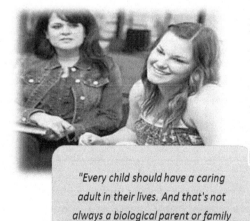

"Every child should have a caring adult in their lives. And that's not always a biological parent or family member. It may be a friend or neighbor. Often times it is a teacher."

Joe Manchin

"Adults sometimes think children don't think. That's what propels them to order children around. But children do integrate thoughts and make sense of them. When I was a child, I thought about everything in the universe."

T'Keyah Crystal Keymah

FOOD FOR THOUGHT

Adventure

Today is a special day.

Today you become an adult.

Today you leave childhood behind.

Today you start a new adventure.

May your path always be open.

May the clouds part from the sun.

May your life be filled with love.

And may you prosper in all you do.

Unknown

WHAT YOU SHOULD KNOW

Cares, thoughts, concerns and behaviors that characterize your world

Cares, thoughts, concerns and behaviors that characterize adults in your world

Some things that you have in common with the adults in your world

ACTIVITY: 1.2 ADULT WORLD

Name:	Date:

Identify a caring adult in your life (hint go back to your HEROES list). Share the list you created during the activity in the YOUR WORLD unit. Ask that same caring adult to give you a glimpse into their world and their perspective by sharing things that are important to them. Being open and honest provides you with a list of their cares, thoughts, concerns, and behaviors previously discussed.

Responses	
1.	2.
3.	4.
5.	6.
7.	8.
9.	10.
11.	12.
13.	14.
15.	16.
17.	18.
19.	20.
21.	22.
23.	24.
25.	26.
27.	28.
29.	30.
31.	32.

1.3 MAKING THE COMPARISON

In this unit, you will observe and record the immediate cares, thoughts, concerns and behaviors that fill your world. The two of you should work together. This information will be used to compare and contrast your world with that of adults.

NONCOGNITIVE VARIABLE(S)

- **AVAILABILITY OF STRONG SUPPORT PERSON:** Seeks and takes advantage of a strong support network or has someone to turn to in a crisis or for encouragement.

- **REALISTIC SELF-APPRAISAL:** Recognizes and accepts any strengths and deficiencies, especially academic, and works hard at self-development. Recognizes need to broaden individuality.

LESSON

The adult world is about planning, producing, looking to the future and being prepared to achieve desired results. Your world is different. You are often fixated on the present, focusing on what works for the moment and going from one fun, fascinating event to the next one. It is true that the two worlds can be vastly different, or at least it seems that way on the surface. Let's compare the different worlds. Both you and your caring adult will work together to compare and contrast each other's individual worlds.

Youth & Adult Common Ground

Well-being - safety, health, and the provision of needs

Joy - happiness, sharing with family and friends, pleasure in what we have

Success - progressive realization of a worthy idea

FOOD FOR THOUGHT

Wiser Than You

People who are successful consult with people who are older because they know that they have had more experiences. Those individuals who have been where you want to go can give you invaluable information. They can not only share with you what they did, but they can also tell you what they did not do, and wish they would have done. People who are older than you have the unique viewpoint of having traveled a road that you have yet to travel and you can take advantage of their vast experiences.

It has been said that a new broom may sweep well, but an old broom knows the corners. Therefore, to be well rounded, you will need to take advantage of your peers' experiences and more so the vast experiences of wiser adults.

In traditional societies, elders always hold positions of respect because of the vast amount of experience they have gained throughout their lives. Use this experience to your advantage. Stand on the shoulder of these giants. Spend time with people who are older and wiser than you and learn from their experiences.

Anonymous

WHAT YOU SHOULD KNOW

How your world and adult world are different

How your world and adult world are alike

Three common threads that connect youth and adult worlds

ACTIVITY: 1.3 MAKING THE COMPARISON

Name:	Date:

Using your "my world" and "adult world" lists your caring adult completed and shared with you previously, compare and record your worlds on the Alike-and-Different chart below.

How are the worlds alike?	How are the worlds different?
What are some things youth and adults have in common?	What are some things that youth and adults do not have in common?
1.	
2.	
3.	
4.	
5.	
6.	
7.	
8.	
9.	
10.	
11.	
12.	
13.	
14.	
15.	
16.	

1.4 THE TWO WORLDS MEET

Now that you have had a chance to review the two worlds, it may seem that you and adults at times seem to live in two different worlds. You are focusing on those things that are relevant and important to you while coexisting in a world with adults focusing on those things that are equally relevant and important to them. The two worlds exist, and that is what creates the great divide.

NONCOGNITIVE VARIABLE(S)

- **AVAILABILITY OF STRONG SUPPORT PERSON:** Seeks and takes advantage of a strong support network or has someone to turn to in a crisis or for encouragement.

- **REALISTIC SELF-APPRAISAL:** Recognizes and accepts any strengths and deficiencies, especially academic, and works hard at self-development. Recognizes need to broaden individuality.

LESSON

Have you ever heard an older person say do not burn bridges because you may have to cross that bridge again? The important message behind that adage is that you should try to maintain good relationships. Good relationships can help you accomplish goals and are the foundation for success in life. Respect, communication and caring are three key elements every business, personal, and family relationship needs in order to be successful. You and your caring adult will develop a list of additional key elements that must be in place to establish and maintain a healthy relationship. Together you will establish a framework for a healthy RELATIONSHIP, which can build a bridge that brings your worlds together.

Find someone who knows you are not perfect but treats you as if you are!

FOOD FOR THOUGHT

Often the adult book is not for you, not yet, or will only be for you when you're ready. But sometimes you will read it anyway, and you will take from it whatever you can. Then, perhaps, you will come back to it when you're older, and you will find the book has changed because you have changed as well, and the book is wiser, or more foolish, because you are wiser or more foolish than you were as a child.

Neil Gaiman

The Truth?

I like you.
A lot.
You make me happy.
You make me laugh.
You're smart.
You're different.
You're a little crazy,
and awkward,
and your smile alone can make my day.

Anonymous

WHAT YOU SHOULD KNOW

The divide that sometimes exists between your world and the adult world

The common ground that both you and adults share

Some necessary ingredients for achieving great relationships

ACTIVITY: 1.4 THE TWO WORLDS MEET

Name:	Date:

As you continue to grow, your **relationships** will be the basis and foundation for success. At any time, should you feel any element of your relationship has been violated, stop and revisit your list. Refer back to your list and identify the specific element violated, talk about the violation and discuss what should be done to correct it. Always remember the *Faces of Change 2* tagline, "Assume Nothing!" As you continue to grow and mature, you will discover new elements to add to this list. Feel free to add elements as you advance through the *Faces of Change 2* process together.

In the space provided, list ten or more additional elements the two of you agree upon that must be in place to establish and maintain a good relationship.

Strong Relationships Yield Results

1. Communication	2. Respect
3. Caring	4.
5.	6.
7.	8.
9.	10.
11.	12.
13.	14.
15.	16.

1.5 SUCCESS AND FAILURE

Have you planned and prepared for your future? If not, you probably will not make it to your desired destination. Most people don't wake up in the morning and say they want to spend the rest of their life in poverty or that they do not want to graduate from high school. Instead, it is a failure to plan that leads to many bad situations in life.

NONCOGNITIVE VARIABLE(S)

- **REALISTIC SELF-APPRAISAL:** Recognizes and accepts any strengths and deficiencies, especially academic, and works hard at self-development. Recognizes need to broaden individuality.

- **PREFERS LONG-RANGE TO SHORT-TERM OR IMMEDIATE NEEDS:** Able to respond to deferred gratification; plans ahead and sets goals.

- **POSITIVE SELF-CONCEPT:** Demonstrates confidence, strength of character, determination, and independence.

LESSON

"IT IS NOT THE PLAN THAT FAILS IT IS THE FAILURE TO PLAN!"

"The price of success is hard work, dedication to the job at hand, and the determination that whether we win or lose, we have applied the best of ourselves to the task at hand."

Vince Lombardi

"Success is not final, failure is not fatal: it is the courage to continue that counts."

SUCCESS DIAGRAM

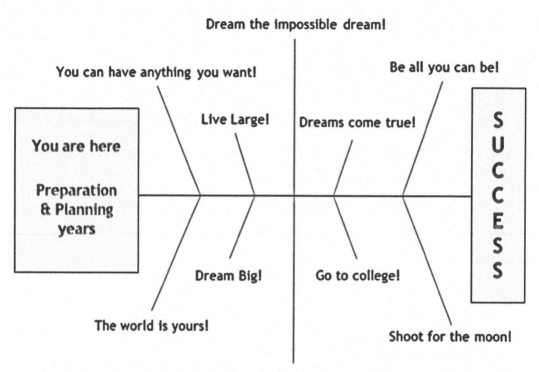

The statements on the diagram above are statements you tend to hear from adults. They use them to encourage and help you along the way, and to keep you moving forward towards your goals in life. Sometimes, however, adults assume they know exactly what you must do to achieve your goals, and their assumptions can be different from yours.

FAILURE DIAGRAM

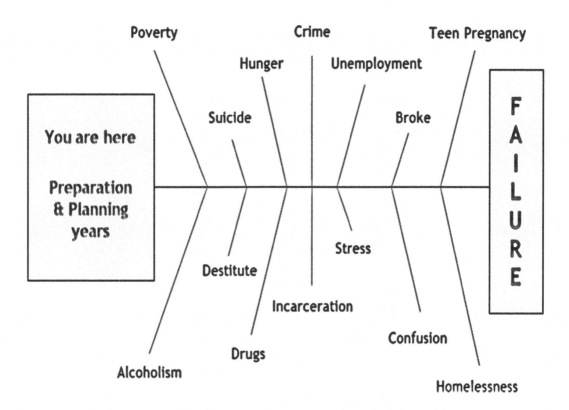

Most people don't wake up in the morning and say, "I am going to strive for failure today. I think I will spend the rest of my life in poverty because I am not going to graduate from high school." Unfortunately, many end up failing simply because they failed to plan.

FOOD FOR THOUGHT

Success and Failure

I do not think all **Failure's** undeserved,

And all **Success** is merely someone's luck;

Some men are down because they were unnerved,

And some are up because they kept their pluck.

Some men are down because they chose to shirk;

Some men are high because they did their work.

I do not think that all the poor are good,

That riches are the uniform of shame;

The beggar might have conquered if he would,

And that he begs, the world is not to blame.

Misfortune is not all that comes to mar;

Most men, themselves, have shaped the things they are.

Edgar Albert Guest

WHAT YOU SHOULD KNOW

Elements that could negatively affect your future success

Elements that can positively affect your future success

The need to plan a successful future

ACTIVITY: 1.5 SUCCESS AND FAILURE

Name:	Date:

What is your definition of **SUCCESS**?

Who do you consider to be successful in life? What do they do for a living? What makes them successful?		
Person	Career	Success
1.		
2.		
3.		
When will you be successful?		

What is your definition of **FAILURE**?

Who do you consider to be a failure? What do they do for a living? Why do you view them as failures?		
Person	Career	Failure
1.		
2.		
3.		
What is your greatest fear?		

1.5.0 FIRST GREATEST DAY

As mentioned in previous units, part of planning and preparing for success is writing down where it is you want to go in life. Writing down the goals you want provides a visual reference point to revisit when needed. It is much easier to keep moving toward your goals when you have them clearly in your sights. If they're not written down, it is much easier to get sidetracked, possibly delayed, and even completely derailed.

NONCOGNITIVE VARIABLE(S)

- **REALISTIC SELF-APPRAISAL:** Recognizes and accepts any strengths and deficiencies, especially academic, and works hard at self-development. Recognizes need to broaden individuality.

- **PREFERS LONG-RANGE TO SHORT-TERM OR IMMEDIATE NEEDS:** Able to respond to deferred gratification; plans ahead and sets goals.

- **POSITIVE SELF-CONCEPT:** Demonstrates confidence, strength of character, determination, and independence.

LESSON

You will now review the aspect of the Faces of Change Timeline known as, "First Greatest Day of My Life - The Day I Was Born" it can be located in the top left-hand corner of your *Faces of Change* Timeline. It has been said, the first gift that you were given was life. Hence, making the day you were born the first greatest day of your life.

No one has your same fingerprints or your deoxyribonucleic (DNA). These are two things that make you completely unique. While others may share the same birthdate and some the same name as you, only you have the unique combination of birthdate, name and DNA.

"FIRST GREATEST DAY OF MY LIFE
WAS THE DAY I WAS BORN!"

BIRTHDATE

The date on which you were born is commonly referred to as your birthdate. In most cases, you share your birthdate with hundreds of other people. The date in itself is not exclusive to you. You are usually given your name on the same day you are born.

NAME

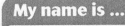

A name can be given to a person, place, or thing. For example, parents can give their child a name or a scientist gives an element a name. Name is term used for identification. Your name uniquely identifies you. Although some, a few or none may share your same name, you are the only you.

DNA

BIOCHEMISTRY
Deoxyribonucleic acid is a self-replicating material present in nearly all living organisms. It is the carrier of genetic information, the fundamental and distinctive characteristics or qualities of someone or something, especially when regarded as unchangeable.

BIRTH DATE + NAME + DNA = YOU!!!

FOOD FOR THOUGHT

Footprints

Walking in the sand

Seems so bland

Leaving footprints where we stand

It doesn't matter what we say.

It will all get washed away

But it's our DNA

It's in memories.

In the stories that hides our queries

The little one

That will run when we are done

The footprints in the sand

Of a little boy's hand

Who will grow up to be a man

Anonymous

Your Name

You got it from your father,
t'was the best he had to give,
And right gladly he bestowed it
It's yours, the while you live.

You may lose the watch he gave
you and another you may claim,
But remember, when you're tempted,
to be careful of his name.

It was fair the day you got it,
and a worthy name to bear,
When he took it from his father
there was no dishonor there.

Through the years he proudly wore it,
to his father he was true,
And that name was clean and spotless
when he passed it on to you.

Oh there's much that he has given
that he values not at all,
He has watched you break your playthings
in the days when you were small.

You have lost the knife he gave you
and you've scattered many a game,
But you'll never hurt your father
if you're careful with his name.

It is yours to wear forever,
yours to wear the while you live,
Yours, perhaps some distant morn,
another boy to give.

And you'll smile as did your father,
with a smile that all can share,
If a clean name and a good name
you are giving him to wear.

Edgar A Guest

WHAT YOU SHOULD KNOW

The need to write down your goals

Identify the first greatest day of your life and explain why

What makes you a one of a kind individual

ACTIVITY: 1.5.0 FIRST GREATEST DAY

Name:	Date:

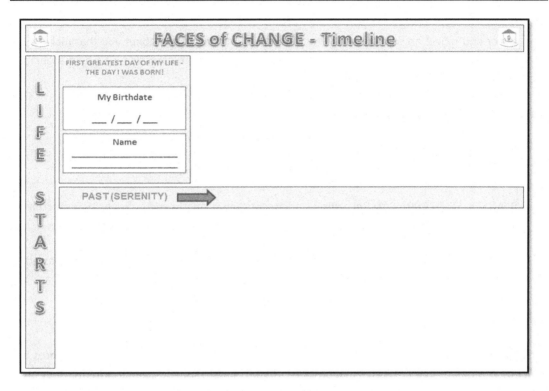

Your name, along with your birthdate, DNA, and personality make you a unique individual, but more importantly one of a kind. While others may share the same name or birthdate, only you have the unique combination of these elements and that makes you special.

Part 1 - Make a copy of the *Faces of Change 2* Timeline on page 19. Then complete the following task in the box labeled, First Greatest Day of My Life:

- Write your birthdate in the space provided on your timeline.

- Write your full name, no nicknames, in the appropriate space on your timeline.

Part 2 - Complete additional tasks below.

- Investigate the origins of your name.

- Are you named after anybody and why?

- Are there any unique stories or events that happened the same day you were born?

- Are there other people in your family who have the same name?

1.5.1 WHO AM I? – SELF-ASSESSMENT

During this unit, you will take time to look inward to assess how you view and what you really think about yourself. After you complete your self-assessments, you will write "I am" statements to continue to discover who you as part of the *Faces of Change 2* process. Take a moment to look in the mirror and reflect on who you are. What are those intimate things about you that make you unique? Next you will be ready to think inwardly and complete an assessment to help evaluate your interests, attributes, and abilities.

NONCOGNITIVE VARIABLE(S)

- **AVAILABILITY OF STRONG SUPPORT PERSON:** Seeks and takes advantage of a strong support network or has someone to turn to in a crisis or for encouragement.

- **REALISTIC SELF-APPRAISAL:** Recognizes and accepts any strengths and deficiencies, especially academic, and works hard at self-development. Recognizes need to broaden individuality.

- **PREFERS LONG-RANGE TO SHORT-TERM OR IMMEDIATE NEEDS:** Able to respond to deferred gratification; plans ahead and sets goals.

LESSON

This unit will serve as a more detailed format for completing the "Who Am I" unit of the *Faces of Change 2* Timeline. You are a culmination of all of your skills, gifts, and talents, whether they are innate, learned or trained. An important step in the process of planning and preparing for success is looking at the past and present so you can design your future. You will take time to do some of this while working on the *Faces of Change 2* Timeline.

WHO

AM

I?

FOOD FOR THOUGHT

Myself

I have to live with myself and so
I want to be fit for myself to know,
I want to be able as days go by,
To look at myself straight in the eye.
I don't want to stand with the setting sun
And hate myself for the things I've done.

I want to go with my head erect,
I want to deserve all men's respect
And in this struggle for fame and pelf
I want to be able to like myself.
I don't want to look at myself and know
That I am a bluster and empty show.

I don't want to hide on a closet shelf
A lot of secrets about myself,
And fool myself as I come and go
Into thinking that nobody else will know
What kind of man I really am;
I don't want to dress myself in sham.

I cannot hide myself from me;
I can see what others can never see;
I know what others can never know,
I cannot fool myself, and so
Whatever happens, I want to be
Self-respecting and conscience free.

Edgar A. Guest

WHAT YOU SHOULD KNOW

Your interests, attributes, and abilities

"I am" statements about yourself

How your past and who you are can influence your choices and decisions

ACTIVITY: 1.5.1 WHO AM I? – SELF-ASSESSMENT

Name:	Date:

Interview yourself for this assessment. There are no right or wrong answers, only answers that are true reflections of you. Take a moment to look in the mirror and reflect on who you are. What are those intimate things about you that make you who you are? The assessment below will help you evaluate your interests, attributes, and abilities. Take the time to think inwardly as you complete this assessment. This will help you start to figure out who you are.

I LOVE . . .

I LIKE . . .

I VALUE . . .

I FEAR . . .

MY TALENTS ARE . . .

I ENJOY . . .

I AM KNOWN FOR . . .

I AM PROUD OF . . .

I SEE MYSELF AS . . .

OTHERS DESCRIBE ME AS . . .

MY STRENGTHS ARE . . .

I NEED TO WORK ON . . .

Now that you have spent some time assessing your interests, attributes, and abilities, review the answers you provided on the self-assessment. Using the self-assessment, complete the "I Am" statements below (e.g. I am a good science student; I am outgoing).

I AM . . .

I AM . . .

I AM . . .

I AM . . .

I AM . . .

I AM . . .

I AM . . .

I AM . . .

I AM . . .

1.5.2 WHO AM I? – S.W.O.T. ANALYSIS

You have already started to map out where you want to go in life, as well as what you want to have, do, and be. Now you have to begin to move from where you are now and work towards where you want to be. You have to transform from the person you are now into the successful adult you can be.

NONCOGNITIVE VARIABLE(S)

- **AVAILABILITY OF STRONG SUPPORT PERSON:** Seeks and takes advantage of a strong support network or has someone to turn to in a crisis or for encouragement.

- **REALISTIC SELF-APPRAISAL:** Recognizes and accepts any strengths and deficiencies, especially academic, and works hard at self-development. Recognizes need to broaden individuality.

- **PREFERS LONG-RANGE TO SHORT-TERM OR IMMEDIATE NEEDS:** Able to respond to deferred gratification; plans ahead and sets goals.

LESSON

The **S.W.O.T.** strategy can be used to help you achieve excellence through self-work. You have to be able to evaluate and actively improve yourself. This is not homework but self-work. Companies and organizations do this all the time in order to stay healthy and productive. **S.W.O.T.** is an acronym that comes out of business. What each letter stands for is explained here and in the picture to the left. They first assess strengths and weaknesses. Any weak areas that are found means self-work must be done. The company then seeks opportunities to improve or correct those weak areas by formulating a plan and then executing it. Lastly they evaluate any threats that may hinder forward progress so they can prepare to confront them as they arise. This way the ongoing work of cultivating excellence is always moving forward.

Conducting a **S.W.O.T.** assessment will be taking another step toward self-evaluation. It will identify areas that need work so you can then formulate a correction plan to achieve greatness.

S.W.O.T. analysis is a useful technique for understanding your Strengths and Weaknesses, and identifying both the Opportunities open to you and the Threats you face. What makes **S.W.O.T.** particularly powerful is it can help you uncover opportunities so you can capitalize on them. And by **understanding** your Weaknesses, you can manage and eliminate Threats.

Moreover, by looking at yourself using the **S.W.O.T.** framework, you can start to craft a strategy that helps you distinguish and position yourself for success in the global market.

Again, as you complete this exercise you are working on the "A Look In the Mirror" section of your *Faces of Change 2* Timeline. Your **S.W.O.T.** analysis will not fit on your timeline. The intent is that you take a closer look at who you are.

S.W.O.T

Consider your **STRENGTHS** from both an internal perspective and from the point of view of other people.
- What advantages do you have?
- What do you do better than anyone else?
- What unique or low-cost resources can you draw upon that others can't?
- What do people see as your strengths?
- What factors mean that you "are the best "?
- What do you do well?
- What are some of your good attributes or qualities?

Again, consider this from an internal and external basis. Do other people seem to perceive **WEAKNESSES** that you don't see? It's best to be realistic now and face any unpleasant truths as soon as possible.
- What could you improve?
- What should you avoid?
- What are people likely to see as weaknesses?
- What do you struggle with?

When looking at **OPPORTUNITIES** look at your strengths and ask yourself whether these open up any avenues. Look at your weaknesses and ask yourself whether you could open up opportunities by eliminating them.
- What good opportunities can you spot?
- What interesting trends are you aware of?
- What resources are available to help you improve your weak area(s)?
Useful opportunities can come from such things as:
- Changes in technology on both a broad and narrow scale.
- Changes in social patterns, lifestyle changes, local events, and so on.

THREATS generally relate to external factors.
- What obstacles do you face?
- What are your competitors doing?
- Is changing technology threatening you?
- Could any of your weaknesses seriously threaten you?
- What or who could hinder your progress towards excellence?

FOOD FOR THOUGHT

Good, better, best.

Never let it rest.

'Til your good is better

and your better is best.

St. Jerome

WHAT YOU SHOULD KNOW

Define self-work

Identify their strengths, weaknesses, opportunities, and threats

Recognize areas where they need to perform self-work

ACTIVITY: 1.5.2 WHO AM I? – S.W.O.T. ANALYSIS

Name:	Date:

	STRENGTHS - attributes, qualities or skills you are good at and do well	
	1.	5.
	2.	6.
	3.	7.
	4.	8.
	WEAKNESSES - qualities or skills you are weak at or need to improve	
	1.	5.
	2.	6.
	3.	7.
	4.	8.
	OPPORTUNITIES - resources available to help you improve	
	1.	5.
	2.	6.
	3.	7.
	4.	8.
	THREATS - factors that could keep you from progressing	
	1.	5.
	2.	6.
	3.	7.
	4.	8.

1.6 YOUTH IN YOUR LIFE – ADULT ASSESSMENT

During this unit, you will have a caring adult assess how they view you. After they complete their assessment, they will write "He/She Is . . ." statements so you can continue to discover how others perceive you as a part of the *Faces of Change 2* process. This step will provide more insight into realizing who you are.

NONCOGNITIVE VARIABLE(S)

- **AVAILABILITY OF STRONG SUPPORT PERSON:** Seeks and takes advantage of a strong support network or has someone to turn to in a crisis or for encouragement.

- **REALISTIC SELF-APPRAISAL:** Recognizes and accepts any strengths and deficiencies, especially academic, and works hard at self-development. Recognizes need to broaden individuality.

- **PREFERS LONG-RANGE TO SHORT-TERM OR IMMEDIATE NEEDS:** Able to respond to deferred gratification; plans ahead and sets goals.

LESSON

This unit will serve as a more detailed format for completing the "Who Am I" unit of the *Faces of Change 2 Timeline.* You are a sum of all of your skills, gifts, and talents whether they are innate, learned or trained. An important step in the process of planning and preparing for success is looking at the past and present so you can design your future.

FACES of CHANGE - Timeline

L I F E S T A R T S

PAST (SERENITY)

LOOK IN THE MIRROR

Who am I?

1. _____

2. _____

How will my past and who I am now impact my future?

Choices _____

Decisions _____

FOOD FOR THOUGHT

Through My Eyes

You are beautiful.

Although, you may not see

the person that I see when I look at you.

And if the mirror you look into

could show your reflection through my eyes

you would see a smile so bright

it could light up the world

throughout the day and into the night.

You are courageous.

Although, you may not feel all that brave.

But I see, how strong you can be

And if you could take a minute

to look back at all your ups and downs

you would smile with pride

because you made it through

And then you would believe

what I already know to be true.

You are incredible,

intelligent fearless and strong.

Life is beautiful, wonderful and fun

and all your dreams can come true

if you start by believing in you.

Anonymous

WHAT YOU SHOULD KNOW ABOUT YOUTH

Assess their interests, attributes, and abilities

Give at least three "I am" statements about them

Explain how their past and who they are can influence their choices and decisions

ACTIVITY: 1.6 YOUTH IN YOUR LIFE – ADULT ASSESSMENT

Name:	Date:

How well do you really know this young person in your life? Take a few moments to assess the young person. Complete the phrases below to help you form a picture of this particular young person. What are the innate attributes that make this person who they are? Try to answer these questions to the best of your knowledge, as honestly and truthful as possible.

He/she loves . . . (E.G. To go shopping)

He/she dislikes . . .

He/she values . . .

He/she fears . . .

His/her talents are . . .

He/she enjoys . . .

He/she is known for . . .

I'm proud of him/her because . . .

I see him/her as…

Others describe him/her as . . .

His/her strengths are . . .

He/she needs to work on . . .

Review the answers you provided in Part I of this young person's innate interests, attributes, and abilities. Using those attributes, and abilities, complete several statements you would use to describe this person below (e.., he/she is a talented artist; he/she never talks with strangers).

He/She Is . . .

He/She Is . . .

He/She Is . . .

He/She Is . . .

He/She Is . . .

He/She Is . . .

He/She Is . . .

He/She Is . . .

He/She Is . . .

He/She Is . . .

1.7 OUR DEEPEST FEAR

During this unit, you and your caring adult will compare and discuss how you view yourself and also how the caring adult views you. After they complete their "He/She Is . . ." statements about you, the two of you can continue to discuss how others perceive you as a part of the *Faces of Change 2* process. This step will allow more inward thinking.

NONCOGNITIVE VARIABLE(S)

- **AVAILABILITY OF STRONG SUPPORT PERSON**: Seeks and takes advantage of a strong support network or has someone to turn to in a crisis or for encouragement.

- **REALISTIC SELF-APPRAISAL:** Recognizes and accepts any strengths and deficiencies, especially academic, and works hard at self-development. Recognizes need to broaden his/her individuality.

- **PREFERS LONG-RANGE TO SHORT-TERM OR IMMRDIATE NEEDS:** Able to respond to deferred gratification, plans ahead and sets goals.

LESSON

No One

No one cares what I think,
No one hears what I speak.
No one tries to understand,
Nor dares to believe.
A very good listener,
But no one listens to me.

Clovis

FOOD FOR THOUGHT

Our Deepest Fear

"Our deepest fear is not that we are inadequate.

Our deepest fear is that we are powerful beyond measure.

It is our light, not our darkness that most frightens us.

We ask ourselves, who am I to be brilliant, gorgeous, talented, fabulous?

Actually, who are you not to be?

You are a child of God.

Your playing small does not serve the world.

There is nothing enlightened about shrinking so that other people won't feel insecure around you.

We are all meant to shine, as children do.

We were born to make manifest the glory of God that is within us.

It's not just in some of us; it's in everyone.

And as we let our own light shine, we unconsciously give other people permission to do the same.

As we are liberated from our own fear, our presence automatically liberates others."

Marianne Williamson

WHAT YOU SHOULD KNOW

Assess your interests, attributes, and abilities

Give at least three "I am" statements about you

Explain how your past and who you are can influence your choices and decisions

ACTIVITY: 1.7 OUR DEEPEST FEAR

Name:	Date:

Now that you both have spent some time assessing interests, attributes, and abilities, take a moment to compare your assessments. Compare the statements that you both created as well. What are some of the assessments that the two of you share?

1.
2.
3.

Did the two of you differ in opinion? If so, in what areas? Why do you think this is?

1.
2.
3.

How might comparing the two assessments help in building a good relationship between the two of you? (e.g. It could help your caring adult understand more about the interests that you have.)

1.
2.
3.

1.8 SECOND GREATEST DAY – DISCOVERY

You will continue to use the *Faces of Change 2* Timeline to chart your progress towards a successful adulthood. In this unit, you will identify what the Second Greatest Day of your life is! You may already know right now what it is you are here to do and what you were born to do. Others are still working to figure it out. The point to remember is that we all are uniquely created for a unique purpose. Throughout this process, we will work to discover what that purpose is.

NONCOGNITIVE VARIABLE(S)

- **AVAILABILITY OF STRONG SUPPORT PERSON:** Seeks and takes advantage of a strong support network or has someone to turn to in a crisis or for encouragement.

- **REALISTIC SELF-APPRAISAL:** Recognizes and accepts any strengths and deficiencies, especially academic, and works hard at self-development. Recognizes need to broaden individuality.

- **PREFERS LONG-RANGE TO SHORT-TERM OR IMMEDIATE NEEDS:** Able to respond to deferred gratification; plans ahead and sets goals.

LESSON

It is human nature for us all to ask questions. We are curious people and have the cognitive capacity for reason and logic. One of the questions that everyone asks at some point in their development is, "Why am I here?" This is a unique question because it is one that each individual must answer for himself/herself. How you answer this question will ultimately shape and determine your future direction.

There are several different ways you can or will discover what you are truly meant to do in life. There is one thing for certain: once you discover what it is, there is nothing that can stop you from achieving it. Your discovery can come from one of three avenues.

You will begin to take a look at three factors that must be considered as you begin to prepare for life.

CAREER AGE

24 represents your "Career Age". This is the age by which most individuals have entered the workforce and/or their chosen career. By age 24 you will be living on your own and will be responsible for yourself with little to no reliance on your parent/guardian or other adults.

MY AGE

As presented in the Introduction to Timeline unit, "My Age" is captured in the **PRESENT** section, meaning the period of time now occurring, the present choices and actions you take will determine your future. Also, having **COURAGE** is the ability to do something that frightens you. Courage allows you to take full advantage of the moments you have right now and plan for a great future.

WHAT YOU DO TODAY CAN IMPROVE ALL YOUR TOMORROWS

CAREER PREPARATION

LIFE PREPARATION YEARS

Represents the time you have to prepare for adulthood. This is the number of years you will have to acquire all of the skills and knowledge needed to be a self-sufficient adult.
Most of your formal education will take place
in these years. You will more than likely move into your first home away from your parent(s). When you see the actual number of years you have to prepare for life, it should become very clear that you do not have time to waste. After all, you are getting ready for the rest of your life.

DISCOVER, WHY YOU WERE BORN!

to see, find, or become aware of (something) for the first time

to show the presence of (something hidden or difficult to see)

DEFINITIONS

to make (something) known

to learn or find out (something surprising or unexpected)

PASSION
a strong feeling of enthusiasm or excitement for something or about doing something

PURPOSE
the reason why something is done or used: the aim or intention of something

CATEGORIES

INNATE
existing from the time a person or animal is born

OBSERVE
to watch and sometimes also listen to (someone or something) carefully

ACTIVITY: 1.8 SECOND GREATEST DAY – DISCOVERY

Name:	Date:

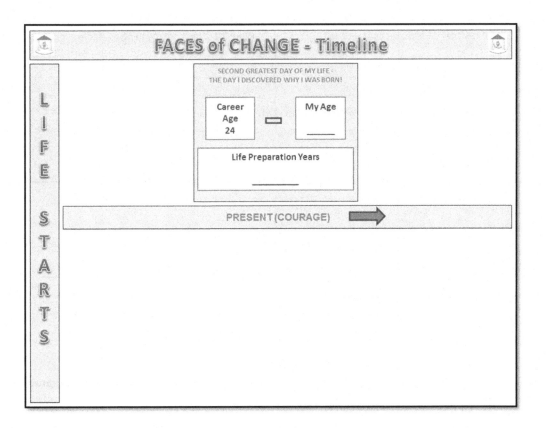

CALCULATE below. Then insert information on Faces of Change 2 Timeline in space shown above.

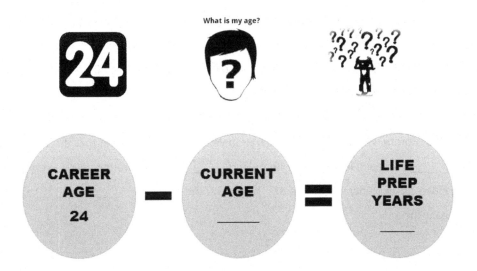

DISCOVER WHY YOU WERE BORN!

Using one or more of the categories below, create your Discovery List!

PASSION - What makes you feel good?

1. _____
2. _____
3. _____
4. _____

PURPOSE - What are the things you enjoy doing?

1. _____
2. _____
3. _____
4. _____

DISCOVERY LIST

INNATE - What are you naturally good at doing?

1. _____
2. _____
3. _____
4. _____

OBSERVATION - What others are doing that interest you?

1. _____
2. _____
3. _____
4. _____

Using the information from the previous units to complete the following **Life Preparation Statement**:

Hello, I my name is _____. I am fully aware of the fact that the first greatest day of my life is the day I was b __ __ __, for without birth nothing else could happen in my life. I also recognize the second greatest day is when I d __ __ __ __ __ __ __ __ __ __ why I was born! My discovery may come from something I o __ __ __ __ __ __ __ someone else doing, an i __ __ __ __ __ __ ability I was born with, a p __ __ __ __ __ __ that creates a strong feeling within me, or knowing my p __ __ __ __ __ __ __ or reason for living is being fulfilled. Adulthood is much longer than childhood. The choices and decisions during these valuable l __ __ __ - p __ __ __ __ __ __ __ __ __ __ __ years will determine the type of life I will live as an adult. I am currently _____ years old; therefore, I have ____ Life Preparation years. I also understand that this time next year I will be _____ years old, leaving me with only _____ life preparation years. Every year I grow older I move closer to my career age of_____. I must have c __ __ __ __ __ __ and not fear planning my future!

1.8.0 SECOND GREATEST DAY – HEADLINES

In this unit, you will take a look into your future and create headlines for your life that address what you will be doing when you reach your career age. You will continue to use the *Faces of Change 2* timeline to chart your progress towards a successful adulthood.

NONCOGNITIVE VARIABLE(S)

- **AVAILABILITY OF STRONG SUPPORT PERSON:** Seeks and takes advantage of a strong support network or has someone to turn to in a crisis or for encouragement.

- **REALISTIC SELF-APPRAISAL:** Recognizes and accepts any strengths and deficiencies, especially academic, and works hard at self-development. Recognizes need to broaden individuality.

- **PREFERS LONG-RANGE TO SHORT-TERM OR IMMEDIATE NEEDS:** Able to respond to deferred gratification; plans ahead and sets goals.

LESSON

In our world where information is ever present, we cannot help but catch a headline or two a day. Whether it is by television, radio, cell phone, or social media, we seemingly can't escape them. Headlines grab your attention and spark your interest in a story by succinctly giving you the highlights of a larger story. Did you know that there are writers who create headlines as a job? Today you will become a headline writer. You will create the headlines for your own life. Looking down the road at the rest of your life, what do you want your story to be? If you were the focus of a news story, what would your headlines be?

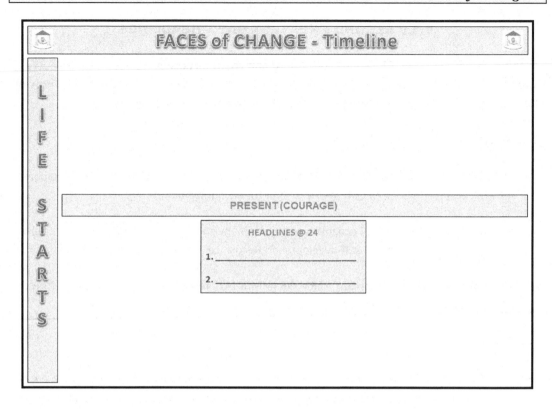

FACES of CHANGE - Timeline

LIFE STARTS

PRESENT (COURAGE)

HEADLINES @ 24

1. _____

2. _____

FOOD FOR THOUGHT

In 1888 Alfred Nobel dropped the newspaper and put his head in his hands. Nobel was a Swedish chemist who had made a fortune inventing and producing dynamite. His brother Ludvig had died in France. Alfred's grief for his brother was made just that much worse as he read the newspaper that morning. He had just read an obituary in a French newspaper – not his brother's obituary, but his own! An editor had confused the brothers. The headline read, "The Merchant of Death is Dead," and it described the life of a man who had gotten rich by helping people kill one another. Alfred was shaken by this assessment of his life and he decided that day to change his legacy. When he died eight years later, he left $9 million to fund awards for people whose work benefited humanity. The award became the Nobel Prize.

WHAT YOU SHOULD KNOW

Your headlines for life

Identify the many accomplishments needed to make your headlines a reality

Understand how planning and preparation can affect accomplishing your HEADLINES

64

ACTIVITY: 1.8.0 SECOND GREATEST DAY – HEADLINES

Name:	Date:

How did Alfred Nobel's headlines impact his life and others?

Why did Alfred Nobel want to change his headlines?

Name three people who have won the Nobel Peace Prize and why.

In the space provided below write your headlines – do not allow anyone else to do that for you!!!

HEADLINE # 1:	GONE VIRAL!
HEADLINE 2:	BREAKING NEWS STORY!
HEADLINE 3:	TODAY'S TOP STORY!!!

What accomplishments would you like to see in your life?
1.

2.

3.

What accomplishments would you like to see in the life of your youth?
1

2

3

2.0 THE ROAD AHEAD – WARM UP

The key to proper growth and movement through the phases of life for you is realizing you are indeed in a race. These phases will help you understand what it takes to keep moving forward toward a healthy, well-adjusted adulthood. Your life is about moving forward, growing and maturing in a positive and fulfilling way. This unit will help you recognize which phase of life you are in and begin to look forward to the phases that are still to come.

NONCOGNITIVE VARIABLE(S)

- **AVAILABILITY OF STRONG SUPPORT PERSON:** Seeks and takes advantage of a strong support network or has someone to turn to in a crisis or for encouragement.

- **REALISTIC SELF-APPRAISAL:** Recognizes and accepts any strengths and deficiencies, especially academic, and works hard at self-development. Recognizes need to broaden individuality.

- **PREFERS LONG-RANGE TO SHORT-TERM OR IMMEDIATE NEEDS:** Able to respond to deferred gratification; plans ahead and sets goals.

LESSON

When we are born into this world, we immediately begin the race of life, constantly moving from one phase of life to another. Unfortunately, adults too often assume that moving forward in age automatically equips youth for the next stage in their maturation process. Progressing forward in age alone does not necessarily equal proper maturation. At each stage in the maturation process, two crucial events happen: skills are mastered and matured, and important choices are made.

"Life is a process of becoming a combination of states

we have to go through. Where people fail is that they

wish to elect a state and remain in it. This is a kind of death."

Anaïs Nin

"Growth is the only evidence of life."

John Henry Newman

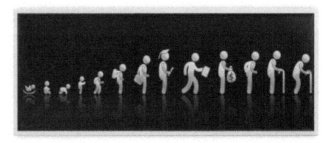

In March, 2004 the Centers for Disease Control (CDC) and Prevention reported the following information:

- 77 years is the average life expectancy for the total US population
- 74.4 years is the average life expectancy for men in the US
- 79.8 years is the average life expectancy for women in the US

FOOD FOR THOUGHT

A Full Life

To live your life to its fullest is your greatest responsibility. You have been given the gift of life. To squander your life is like throwing a way a gift that someone has given you. Those individuals who worry about things that they don't have instead of focusing on things that they do have are said to be majoring in minors. If you pay attention to the good things in your life, you will find yourself living your life to the fullest.

You have a quiver of talent, skills, interests, and aptitudes. Aim towards the thoughts, ideas, values, and visions that will take you toward the goals in your life and will bring you happiness. Follow the path of desire that leads to happiness and fulfillment. Open your mind and your heart to the ideas that enrich your life.

Anonymous

WHAT YOU SHOULD KNOW

Understand that life is about moving through phases

Identify the approximate number of quality years they will have in their life

Recognize the importance of planning and preparing for life

ACTIVITY: 2.0 THE ROAD AHEAD – WARM UP

Name:	Date:

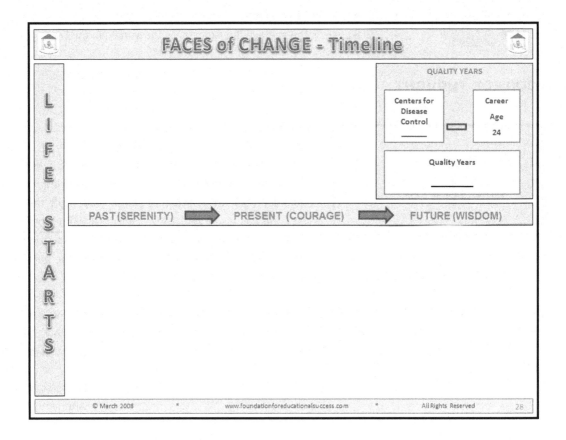

CALCULATE equation below, insert information in your
Faces of Change 2 Timeline illustrated above!

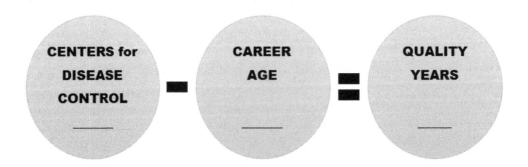

Name five people you know living successful Quality Years? Why do you see them as successful?	Who do you know living unsuccessful Quality Years? Why do you see them as unsuccessful?
NAME: WHY?	NAME: WHY?
NAME: WHY?	NAME: WHY?
NAME: WHY?	NAME: WHY?
NAME: WHY?	NAME: WHY?
NAME: WHY?	NAME: WHY?

2.0.1 WHERE WILL I SHOOT FROM?

Education is no longer an option on the road to success. It is required. Education is a must in order to give yourself the best possible place on the court of life and the best possible chance for future success. Learning increases your earning potential. In the game of life, where will you shoot?

NONCOGNITIVE VARIABLE(S)

- **PREFERS LONG-RANGE TO SHORT-TERM OR IMMEDIATE NEEDS:** Able to respond to deferred gratification; plans ahead and sets goals.

- **REALISTIC SELF-APPRAISAL:** Recognizes and accepts any strengths and deficiencies, especially academic, and works hard at self-development. Recognizes need to broaden individuality.

LESSON

While every choice or decision made can affect the ultimate outcomes you seek in life, none probably make as great an impact than making your education a priority. Your education can either help you or hinder you when it comes to reaching your goals. Having goals is great, but having the proper education or training needed to help make those goals a reality is priceless.

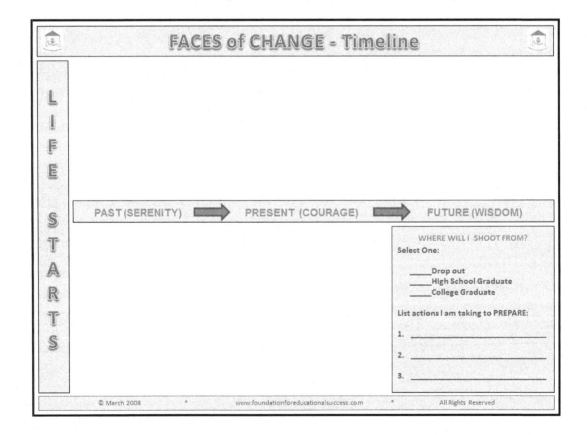

FACES of CHANGE - Timeline

L I F E S T A R T S

PAST (SERENITY) ➡ PRESENT (COURAGE) ➡ FUTURE (WISDOM)

WHERE WILL I SHOOT FROM?
Select One:

_____ Drop out
_____ High School Graduate
_____ College Graduate

List actions I am taking to PREPARE:

1. _____
2. _____
3. _____

© March 2008   *   www.foundationforeducationalsuccess.com   *   All Rights Reserved

FOOD FOR THOUGHT

*85% of current jobs are considered "skilled," requiring education beyond high school,
and 40% of all new jobs will require at least an associate's degree.*

Crisis at the Core. ACT Policy Report, 2004

Equipment

Figure it out for yourself, my lad,
You've all that the greatest of men have had,
Two arms, two hands, two legs, two eyes
And a brain to use if you would be wise.
With this equipment, they all began,
So, start for the top and say, "I can."
Look them over, the wise and great
They take their food from a common plate,
And similar knives and forks they use,
With similar laces, they tie their shoes.
The world considers them brave and smart,
You've all they had when they made their start.
You can triumph and come to skill,
You can be great if you only will.
You're well equipped for what fight you choose,

You have legs and arms and a brain to use,
And the man who has risen great deeds to do
Began his life with no more than you.
You are the handicap you must face,
You are the one who must choose your place,
You must say where you want to go,
How much you will study the truth to know.
God has equipped you for life, but He
Let's you decide what you want to be.
Courage must come from the soul within,
The man must furnish the will to win.
So, figure it out for yourself, my lad.
You were born with all that the great have had,
With your equipment, they all began,
Get hold of yourself and say: "I can."

Edgar A. Guest

WHAT YOU SHOULD KNOW

The importance of making education a priority

Understand that higher education levels place one closer to your goals and a successful career

Understand that lower education levels can hinder progress towards goals and a successful career

ACTIVITY: 2.0.1 WHERE WILL I SHOOT FROM?

Name:	Date:

YOU HAVE TO SHOOT FROM THERE!

Let's take a look at the advantages and disadvantages of being able to shoot from the different spots on the court. Also, imagine being allowed to only shoot from a certain position based on your level of education, which determines how near or far you get to the goal. The goal itself represents great, fantastic, good paying jobs, careers and professions. Remember, as the poem in the Food for Thought section of this unit mentioned you have the same "EQUIPMENT" as the next person! Be sure to carefully read the decision each shooter made regarding their education and/or training, which put them at their prospective positions.

Shooter 3: Dropout, decides to get a job, drop out of high school and not earn a diploma. They would be relegated to shooting from the baseline on the opposite end of the court.

Advantages	Disadvantages
1._____	1._____
2._____	2._____
3._____	3._____

How do you think it feels to shoot from the position of a dropout?

Shooter 2: High School Graduate, decides dropping out is not good enough so to do better they remain in school and earn their high school diploma. This now affords them the right to shoot from anywhere behind half court; but never to cross that line to get closer to the goal, but yet in front of dropouts.

Advantages	Disadvantages
1._____	1._____
2._____	2._____
3._____	3._____

How do you think it feels to shoot from the position of a high school graduate?

Shooter 1: College Graduate, decides to go to college and earn their degree or some form of post-secondary training, certification or military/civil service training. They've earned the right to shoot from anywhere between the free throw line and the goal; always in front of the high school graduates and dropouts.

Advantages	Disadvantages
1._____	1._____
2._____	2._____
3._____	3._____

How do you think it feels to shoot from the position of a college graduate?

Where Will You Shoot From? (check one) Place your response on your *Faces of Change 2* Timeline.

_____ **Dropout**

_____ **High School Graduate**

_____ **College Graduate**

Based on the choice you selected above list as many action steps you can take to prepare for success. Also, list as many of these actions as possible on the space provided on your Timeline. Your caring adult guide, mentor or hero can be very helpful with this list.
Action: (Example: Take my classes more serious by studying more)
Action:
Action:
Action:
Action:
Action:
Action:
Action:
Action:
Action:
Action:
Action:
Action:
Action:
Action:

2.1 TIMES OF MY LIFE

In this unit, you will begin to mark and identify those many milestones you have already achieved, the ones you are working on now, and the future ones. This exercise will serve as a compass to help you navigate your way through life. It will serve as a constant reminder of the great accomplishments you have already made and ones you have yet to achieve.

NONCOGNITIVE VARIABLE(S)

- **PREFERS LONG-RANGE TO SHORT-TERM OR IMMEDIATE NEEDS:** Able to respond to deferred gratification; plans ahead and sets goals.

- **REALISTIC SELF-APPRAISAL:** Recognizes and accepts any strengths and deficiencies, especially academic, and works hard at self-development. Recognizes need to broaden individuality.

LESSON

If you have ever had a history class, I bet you would agree that one thing you can't avoid is learning and memorizing dates. As we study history we sight the times and achievements of people from various periods as they have made their mark in time is part of recognizing history.

You create your own history every day. You have your own achievements and time periods that you are living now. You are going to take some time looking at some of those past, present, and future achievements and occasions. During your progression through life, you will celebrate, recognize, memorialize and mark various significant occasions that will occur. Some of these occasions shape and others guide you through your phases of life.

"There are different kinds of challenges depending upon what phase of life I'm in!"

Alanis Morissette

"I used to think that each phase of life was the end. But now that my view on life is more or less fixed, I believe that change is a great thing. In fact, it's the only real absolute in the world."

Phillip Johnson

FOOD FOR THOUGHT

It's Not What You Don't Have

Circumstances can either make or break us. The choice is ours. You've heard it many times: "Life is what you make it." Or we could put it in a slightly different way, as my friend Ty Boyd does, and say, "You can't change the cards life has dealt you, but you can determine the way you'll play them." That's the philosophy Wendy Stoeker decided to live by. When she was a freshman she placed third in the girls' state diving championship. At that point she was swimming in the number two spot on the highly competitive Florida swim team and carrying a full academic load.

Wendy Stoeker certainly sounds like an accomplished, happy, positive, well-balance coed, capable of making life whatever she wishes it to be, doesn't she? Well, you're right when you say that she was and is. The fact is, she already has made life what she wants it to be, even though she was born without arms.

Despite having no arms, Wendy enjoys bowling and water-skiing, and she types more than forty-five words a minute. Wendy doesn't look down at what she does not have. She looks up at what she does have. The reality is that if all of us would use what we have and not worry about what we don't have, we would be able to accomplish infinitely more in our lives.

The message is this: Follow the example of Wendy Stoeker. Think positively about what you want in life. Determine to use what you have, regardless of the obstacles you might face. If you do that, you will make your life more exciting, rewarding, and productive. Many people itch for what they want, but they won't scratch for it.

Zig Ziglar

WHAT YOU SHOULD KNOW

Recognize you will have momentous occasions in each phase of life

Identify past, present and future momentous occasions

Recognize Faces of Change 2 caring adult as an instrumental helper in your progression through the phases of life

ACTIVITY: 2.1 TIMES OF MY LIFE

Name:	Date:

Following is a Time-Chart for you to record various events in your life. You can include events such as when you started elementary school, when you moved (if you have moved), when you learned to ride a bike, when you learned (or will learn) to drive a car, school graduation, when you will attend and graduate from college, when you will begin work, when you will get married, when you will buy your first house, etc.

- I will complete a timeline for my life, including past, present, and future events of importance in my life.
- I will identify the two most important days in my life and record them on my *Faces of Change 2* timeline as well.

Keep the following points in mind as you complete your Time-Chart:

- Be Realistic
- Be Meaningful
- Be Well-Defined
- Excite You
- Have a Logical Progression
- Fine Tune
- Have Positive Action

Other events to place on your Time-Chart:

What did you identify as the first most important day of your life? If it is not the day you were born, why did you choose this date?

Chart the second most important day in your life on your Time-Chart. Where did you place this day? Why?

2.1 PHASES OF LIFE – TIMES OF MY LIFE
TIME-CHART

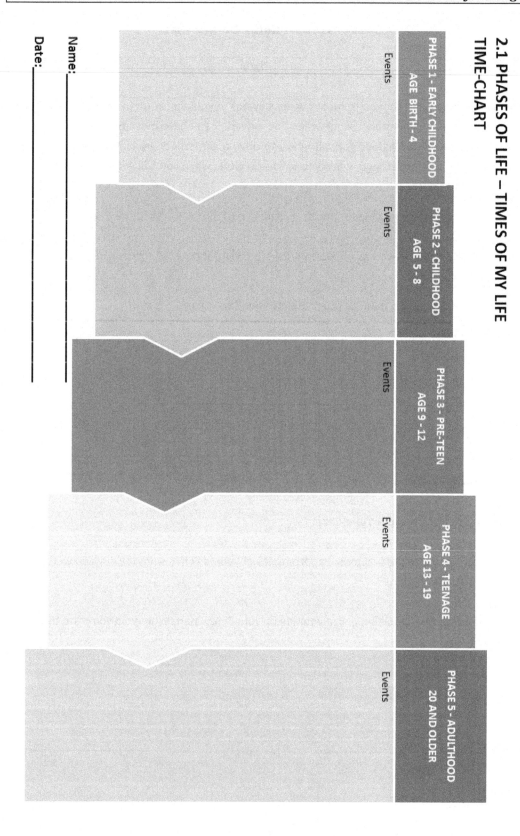

PHASE 1 - EARLY CHILDHOOD AGE BIRTH - 4	Events
PHASE 2 - CHILDHOOD AGE 5 - 8	Events
PHASE 3 - PRE-TEEN AGE 9 - 12	Events
PHASE 4 - TEENAGE AGE 13 - 19	Events
PHASE 5 - ADULTHOOD 20 AND OLDER	Events

Name:

Date:

2.2 MATURATION STATIONS

Each phase of life requires you to gain what you need in it to be prepared for the next one. As you view the time in each of the phases, notice you will spend much more time in your adult phase than you will spend in the first four phases combined.

NONCOGNITIVE VARIABLE(S)

- **REALISTIC SELF-APPRAISAL:** Recognizes and accepts any strengths and deficiencies, especially academic, and works hard at self-development. Recognizes need to broaden individuality.

- **PREFERS LONG-RANGE TO SHORT-TERM OR IMMEDIATE NEEDS:** Able to respond to deferred gratification; plans ahead and sets goals.

LESSON

As you grow older and mature, you will willingly or unwillingly move through several phases of life. Time is always moving, propelling you forward. Have you ever thought about the phases in life you will go through and how much time you spend in them? In this unit, you, will take a look at both.

Ironically, the first four phases of your life are where the majority of your Life Preparation years are. Like it or not, the activities, choices, and decisions you make as a child and teenager will have a direct impact on how you will live your life as an adult. This is why it is so important that as you are enjoying your pre-teen through teen phases you simultaneously plan for your future. You cannot waste time and/or wait until you become an adult if you want to be successful.

EARLY CHILDHOOD	CHILDHOOD	PRE-TEEN	TEEN	ADULTHOOD
Birth – 4	5 – 9	10 – 12	13 – 19	20 – beyond
4 years	5 years	3 years	7 years	Lifetime

Time Well Spent:

Whether conscious (fully aware that it is happening) or subconscious (not fully aware), you will spend your time in various phases experiencing the following factors:

RECREATION	LIVELIHOOD	EXPLORATION:	EDUCATION:	PREPARATION:	MATURATION:
•something people do to relax or have fun; activities done for enjoyment	•a way of earning money to live	• the act or an instance of expressing options	•knowledge, skill, and understanding that you earn or obtain	• the activity or process of making something ready or of becoming ready for something	•the emergence of personal and behavioral characteristics through growth processes

The chart below illustrates how the average person allocates their time while in each phase of life. When you are younger, you do not have a large say on how you will spend your time. As you grow older and mature, you have more control of how you spend your time. When you mature, the way you spend time shifts.

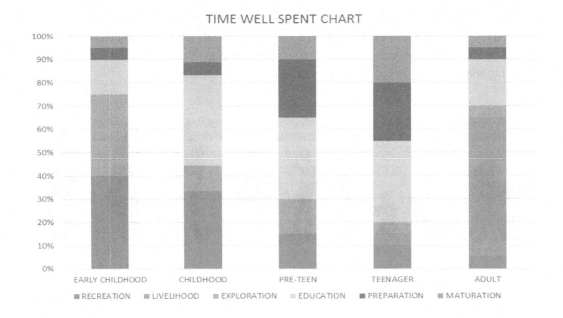

PERCENTAGE OF TIME WELL SPENT

EARLY CHILDHOOD		CHILDHOOD		PRE-TEEN		TEENAGER		ADULTHOOD	
Recreation	40	Recreation	40	Recreation	15	Recreation	10	Recreation	5
Livelihood	0	Livelihood	0	Livelihood	0	Livelihood	5	Livelihood	60
Exploration	35	Exploration	10	Exploration	15	Exploration	5	Exploration	5
Education	15	Education	35	Education	35	Education	35	Education	20
Preparation	5	Preparation	5	Preparation	25	Preparation	25	Preparation	5
Maturation	5	Maturation	10	Maturation	10	Maturation	20	Maturation	5

FOOD FOR THOUGHT

Minute

I have only just a minute,

Only sixty seconds in it.

Forced upon me, can't refuse it.

Didn't seek it,

didn't choose it.

But it's up to me to use it.

I must suffer if I lose it.

Give account if I abuse it.

Just a tiny little minute,

but eternity is in it.

Dr. Benjamin E. Mays

WHAT YOU SHOULD KNOW

The five phases of life

Associate an age range with each phase of life

Recognize adulthood as the longest phase of life

ACTIVITY: 2.2 MATURATION STATIONS

Name:	Date:

EARLY CHILDHOOD	CHILDHOOD	PRE-TEEN	TEEN	ADULTHOOD
Birth – 4	5 – 9	10 – 12	13 – 19	20 – beyond

Which Phase of Life are you currently in? _____

Which phase encompasses the most amount of time in an individual's life? _____

What is the total number of years combined from birth to the start of adulthood? _____

MY TIME WELL SPENT

Create your personal Time Well Spent scale for the phase of life you are in now. Be sure the total adds up to 100%

FACTORS	PERCENTAGE
RECREATION	%
LIVELIHOOD	%
EXPLORATION	%
EDUCATION	%
PREPARATION	%
MATURATION	%

Productive

In your current Phase of Life, list productive ways you spend your time. Next to each way explain how it can significantly impact your future.

Productive Time	Impact
1.	
2.	
3.	
4.	
5.	
6.	
7.	
8.	
9.	

Counter-Productive

In your current Phase of Life, list counter-productive ways you spend your time. Next to each way explain how it can significantly impact your future.

Counter-Productive Time	Impact
1.	
2.	
3.	
4.	
5.	
6.	
7.	
8.	
9.	

2.3 LIFE SKILLS DEVELOPMENT

During this unit, you will identify and list skills that you have developed or will develop as you move forward in this process. Skill development is what you need to properly transition through your phases in life. Progressing through the phases of life is achieved by acquiring necessary skills needed in each phase to progress to the next. Think about the skills you gained (or will gain) during the various phases of your life.

NONCOGNITIVE VARIABLES(S)

- **REALISTIC SELF-APPRAISAL:** Recognizes and accepts any strengths and deficiencies, especially academic, and works hard at self-development. Recognizes need to broaden individuality.

- **PREFERS LONG-RANGE TO SHORT-TERM OR IMMEDIATE NEEDS:** Able to respond to deferred gratification; plans ahead and sets goals.

- **NONTRADITIONAL KNOWLEDGE ACQUIRED:** Acquires knowledge in a sustained and/or culturally related ways in any area, including social, personal, or interpersonal.

LESSON

Developing skills throughout life is continuous. You are constantly developing skills in order to improve. To move from phase to phase and achieve personal growth, you must properly develop each skill. Without proper development, you become stagnant and cannot grow.

In future years as you travel through the various stages of life, you will acquire additional formal and informal skills. One of the characteristics of life for all living organisms is growth and development. As human organisms one of the ways that we grow and develop is by developing different skills.

One of the best examples when describing gaining and developing a skill is learning to ride a bicycle. Mastery came when you could balance yourself, peddle, and steer the bike simultaneously. Maturing occurred when you knew how to ride and knowing when it was a good time to ride (rain or sunshine, day or night, school time or after school, etc.). Stabilizing was when you knew that riding was a recreation and you could only do it when you completed other tasks (e.g. homework, chores, self-improvement, etc.).

Skill Acquisition: development is achieved on three levels:		
1. Mastering:	**2. Maturing:**	**3. Stabilizing:**
ability to easily use new learned skill(s) to succeed; ability to conduct skill(s) without much effort.	ability to practice skill(s) in appropriate manner and situation. This is when you learn when and where.	ability to consistently practice skill(s) appropriately. This is when you subconsciously apply levels 1 & 2.

FOOD FOR THOUGHT

Go Get It

If you want something in life, go get it. Move out from the rationalization of excuses and move on to acquire what you want. Don't depend on others to get it for you. The acquisition of dream and goals is your responsibility.

A man came to America from Eastern Europe and after being processed at Ellis Island went into a cafeteria to get something to eat. He sat down at an empty table and waited for someone to take his order. Of course, nobody did. Finally, a woman with a tray full of food sat down opposite him and informed him how a cafeteria works. "Start at the end," she said, "and go along the line and pick out the food you want. At the other end, they'll tell you how much you have to pay."

Later the man reflected to a new friend on that experience. "I soon learned that's how everything works in America. Life's a cafeteria here. You can get anything you want as long as you are willing to pay the price. But you'll never get what you want if you wait for someone to bring it to you. You have to get up and get it yourself."

You are the only one who can use your ability to reach your goals. You are responsible for moving toward those goals. Your future growth and progress are on your shoulders and in your hands.

The Promise of God's Power for the Graduate

WHAT YOU SHOULD KNOW

Skills learned at each phase of life

The three levels which all skills must be developed

Understand the need to continuously develop skills throughout life

ACTIVITY: 2.3 LIFE SKILLS DEVELOPMENT

Name:	Date:

Part 1: In the space below, begin to create a list of skills you have gained during your various phases of life. As you create your list, keep in mind all those skills that you have gained that made it possible for you to go to the next PHASE OF LIFE.

EARLY CHILDHOOD	CHILDHOOD
1.	1.
2.	2.
3.	3.
4.	4.
5.	5.

PRE-TEENAGER	TEENAGER
1.	1.
2.	2.
3.	3.
4.	4.
5.	5.

ADULTHOOD
1.
2.
3.
4.
5.

Part 2: From your skills list select several skills that you have gained at each phase of life and describe how you have properly taken each through all three levels of development.

Did you know . . . developing skills needed for life is continuous? You always have to work at getting better!

Level 1: **Mastering**		Level 2: **Maturing**		Level 3: **Stabilizing**
• ability to easily use new learned skill(s) to succeed; ability to conduct skill(s) without much effort.	➡	• ability to practice skill(s) in appropriate manner and situation. This is when you learn when and where.	➡	• ability to consistently practice skill(s) appropriately. This is when you subconsciously apply levels 1 & 2.

1. SKILL GAINED:

• Master:

• Mature:

• Stabilize:

2. SKILL GAINED:

• Master:

• Mature:

• Stabilize:

3. SKILL GAINED:

• Master:

• Mature:

• Stabilize:

2.4 CHOICES OF A LIFETIME

In this unit, you will examine the types of choices you make throughout the phases of life and how various influences affect these choices. You will look at some of the choices that you have made and will make in your life as you transition into adulthood. Especially those choices that pertain to your future, influences, and time.

NONCOGNITIVE VARIABLE(S)

- **REALISTIC SELF-APPRAISAL:** Recognizes and accepts any strengths and deficiencies, especially academic, and works hard at self-development. Recognizes need to broaden individuality.

- **NONTRADITIONAL KNOWLEDGE ACQUIRED:** Acquires knowledge in a sustained and/or culturally related ways in any area, including social, personal, or interpersonal.

LESSON

Choices

We all make choices every day. Some of these choices have more impact than others. All choices are impacted by many influences. Whether internal or external sometimes these influences are so subtle that you don't realize how much you are being affected.

Crossroads

As the image to the right illustrates, you will come to crossroads which will cause you to make several choices in life. This is when you must choose which path to take. There are several outside forces that can and will influence the choices you will make once you reach those crossroads. During your progression through life, you will make choices in three areas that will directly affect you later in life:

Future	**Influences**	**Time**
(schooling, employment, relationships, etc.)	(your beliefs and actions)	(improvement or harm; no middle)

Influences

Most young people and many adults don't realize how much is internalized from the ever-present barrage of influences that surround us all. When you are at the crossroads of a choice, what influences you? Many of these influences play a large part in the decisions you will make and will impact your life. In this unit, you will become aware of the everyday influences that surround you. What you take in daily can affect the way you see things and your perceptions.

PEERS	MEDIA	SELF-ESTEEM
SOCIETY	SOCIAL MEDIA	WHAT'S IN IT FOR ME
POPULARITY	LIFE EXPERIENCES	(WIIFM)
ADULTS	FEAR	FAMILY

Media is a huge influence. It is what resonates that can affect us most. Every drama, comedy, music video and reality show is impacting and influencing you. They are each teaching you something.

FOOD FOR THOUGHT

The Road Not Taken

Two roads diverged in a yellow wood,
And sorry I could not travel both
And be one traveler, long I stood
And looked down one as far as I could
To where it bent in the undergrowth;

Then took the other, as just as fair,
And having perhaps the better claim
Because it was grassy and wanted wear;
Though as for that the passing there
Had worn them really about the same,

And both that morning equally lay
In leaves no step had trodden black.
Oh, I kept the first for another day!
Yet knowing how way leads on to way,
I doubted if I should ever come back.

I shall be telling this with a sigh
Somewhere ages and ages hence:
Two roads diverged in a wood, and I—
I took the one less traveled by,
And that has made all the difference.

Robert Frost

WHAT YOU SHOULD KNOW

Identify choices made at each phase of life

Recognize influences in your life

Determine the positive and/or negative impact influences make on your choices in life

ACTIVITY: 2.4 CHOICES OF A LIFETIME

Name:	Date:

Your choices and decisions can affect your development and may possibly affect other choices and decisions you make later in your life.

FACES of CHANGE - Timeline

L I F E S T A R T S

PAST (SERENITY) ➡ PRESENT (COURAGE) ➡ FUTURE (WISDOM)

LOOK IN THE MIRROR

Who am I?

1. _____

2. _____

How will my past and who I am now impact my future?

Choices_____

Decisions_____

© March 2008   *   www.foundationforeducationalsuccess.com   *   All Rights Reserved

---

We all make choices every day. Some of these choices have more impact than others. With the help of your *Faces of Change 2* caring adult, list some choices you made or will make at the various phases of life that can directly affect your life.

EARLY CHILDHOOD

1.

2.

3.

CHILDHOOD

1.

2.

3.

PRE-TEENAGER

1.

2.

3.

TEENAGER

1.

2.

3.

ADULTHOOD

1.

2.

3.

What or who are the major influences in your decision-making process? Why? (e.g. Do you allow images of life that you see portrayed on TV or elsewhere to affect the decisions you make?)

1.	2.
3.	4.
5.	6.
7.	8.
9.	10.
11.	12.
13.	14.
15.	16.

Can influences be positive? How? Can they be negative? How? Take time to discuss this with your caring adult partner.

What are some choices you have already made? (e.g. in childhood you decided how much effort to put into schooling which directly affects later years of schooling and ultimately the type of college and/or job you will be able to choose later in life.)

Future	Control/Influence	Time
1.	1.	1.
2.	2.	2.
3.	3.	3.
4.	4.	4.
5.	5.	5.
6.	6.	6.
7.	7.	7.
8.	8.	8.
9.	9.	9.
10.	10.	10.

List those activities you have been a part of that have helped you grow as a person? (e.g. Taking the time to work through *Faces of Change 2* has helped you see the importance of doing what you can to be ready for the phases of your life.)

1.

2.

3.

4.

5.

6.

7.

8.

List those activities that have been detrimental to your success or harmful to you? (e.g. Not completing my homework assignments, resulting in me not making the best grade I could in a class.)

1.

2.

3.

4.

5.

6.

7.

8.

3.0 MASTER – INTRODUCTION

In this unit, you will review and begin to commit to memory practical skills for self-mastery so that you are prepared to put these skills to practice both now and in the future. The acronym MASTER will serve as a reminder of the list of skills that are needed in order to achieve self-mastery as you transition into adulthood.

NONCOGINITIVE VARIABLE(S)

- **REALISTIC SELF-APPRAISAL:** Recognizes and accepts any strengths and deficiencies, especially academic, and works hard at self-development. Recognizes need to broaden individuality.

- **NONTRADITIONAL KNOWLEDGE ACQUIRED:** Acquires knowledge in a sustained and/or culturally related ways in any area, including social, personal, or interpersonal.

LESSON

When you hear the word "MASTER", many thoughts and images probably come to mind. Some of these may be positive or negative. Maybe you think of those highly-skilled in martial arts who have achieved a certain level of training or you may think of employee/employer relationship with one person having authority over another. One common thread is present whether your images are positive or negative – to MASTER a situation means you have control of it.

Take a look at the diagram below. You will see six skills you need to MASTER in life both professionally and socially. In order to properly transition from phase to phase in life, you must have a command of self – the ability to think and behave in such a way that shows maturation. In this unit, you will look at the six key skills you will need in order to master self and exhibit the traits of a matured adult. Each trait is an excellent practice in and of itself; but when combined, they will transform you into a well-equipped young adult ready for the world.

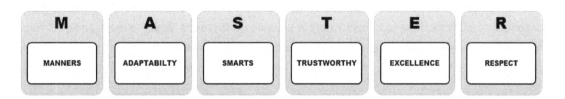

M	A	S	T	E	R
MANNERS	ADAPTABILTY	SMARTS	TRUSTWORTHY	EXCELLENCE	RESPECT

"I've always believed that if you put in the work, the result will come. I don't do things half-heartedly. Because I know if I do, then I can expect half-hearted result."

Michael Jordan

"The ultimate authority must always rest with the individual's own reason and critical analysis."

Dalai Lama

The word MASTER can be used as a noun, a verb, or adjective.		
noun	**verb**	**adjective**
a skilled practitioner of a particular art or activity.	gain control of; overcome.	having or showing very great skill or proficiency.
"I'm a master of disguise"	"I managed to master my fears"	"He is a master painter"

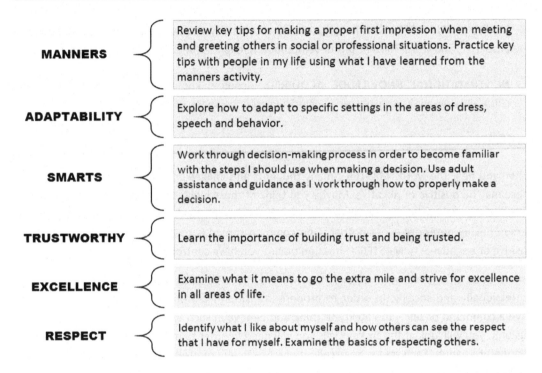

MANNERS — Review key tips for making a proper first impression when meeting and greeting others in social or professional situations. Practice key tips with people in my life using what I have learned from the manners activity.

ADAPTABILITY — Explore how to adapt to specific settings in the areas of dress, speech and behavior.

SMARTS — Work through decision-making process in order to become familiar with the steps I should use when making a decision. Use adult assistance and guidance as I work through how to properly make a decision.

TRUSTWORTHY — Learn the importance of building trust and being trusted.

EXCELLENCE — Examine what it means to go the extra mile and strive for excellence in all areas of life.

RESPECT — Identify what I like about myself and how others can see the respect that I have for myself. Examine the basics of respecting others.

The keys to successfully transitioning into adulthood are self-mastery. Certain life abilities can and must be mastered in your life so you can properly grow and mature socially. These abilities must become a regular practice and a regular part of your life. At first sight for some these abilities seem natural and/or unforced. For others with practice they become just as natural. Being able to be in control of your own life and responsible for your own actions are true marks of becoming an adult.

In this unit, you will:

1. Identify proper social behaviors
2. Comprehend how and when to adapt your behavior to the present situation
3. Acquire a decision-making process
4. Learn the importance of being trustworthy
5. Recognize the need to strive for excellence
6. Understand the importance of respect for others and self

FOOD FOR THOUGHT

Invictus

Out of the night that covers me,

Black as the pit from pole to pole,

I thank whatever gods may be

For my unconquerable soul.

In the fell clutch of circumstance

I have not winced nor cried aloud.

Under the bludgeonings of chance

My head is bloody, but unbowed.

Beyond this place of wrath and tears

Looms but the Horror of the shade,

And yet the menace of the years

Finds, and shall find me, unafraid.

It matters not how strait the gate,

How charged with punishments the scroll,

I am the master of my fate:

I am the captain of my soul.

William Ernest Henley

WHAT YOU SHOULD KNOW

The six skills necessary to master life

Assess your level of mastery for each skill

Recognize which of the skills for life you need to work on

ACTIVITY: 3.0 MASTER – INTRODUCTION

Name:	Date:

Using the scale in the left column below rate how well you conduct each part of M.A.S.T.E.R.

SCALE

5 - Superior
4 - Above average
3 - Average
2 - Fair
1 – Poor

MASTER

_____ Manners
_____ Adaptability
_____ Smarts
_____ Trustworthy
_____ Excellence
_____ Respect

Working It Out...

Working with your caring adult, answer and have a discussion on the questions below. Both you and your caring adult should give an answer to each question.

MANNERS - Based on your knowledge of manners, do you consider yourself a person with good manners (Yes/No Why)?

Youth:

1.

2.

Adult:

1.

2.

ADAPTABILITY - Do you change your behavior for different situations? If so how? What situations require a change in behavior?

Youth:

1.

2.

Adult:

1.

2.

SMARTS - When faced with making decisions, how do you go about making those decisions? What considerations do you take into account? Do you ask for help or guidance?

Youth:

1.

2.

Adult:

1.

2.

TRUSTWORTHY - Would you describe yourself as a person who can be trusted? Why? Would others who know you describe you that way? Why?

Youth:

1.

2.

Adult:

1.

2.

EXCELLENCE - Have you ever found yourself settling for less than what you can do or have? In what areas, have you settled? Why do you settle?

Youth:

1.

2.

Adult:

1.

2.

RESPECT - Do you have respect for yourself and others? How do you show this respect?

Youth:

1.

2.

Adult:

1.

2.

3.1 MANNERS

In this unit, you will be introduced to proper manners and etiquette. You will also review and practice important tips for making a good first impression when meeting and greeting others in social or professional situations.

NONCOGNITIVE VARIABLE(S)

- **REALISTIC SELF-APPRAISAL:** Recognizes and accepts any strengths and deficiencies, especially academic, and works hard at self-development. Recognizes need to broaden individuality.

- **UNDERSTANDS AND KNOWS HOW TO HANDLE THE SYSTEM:** Exhibits a realistic view of the system based upon personal experiences and is committed to improving the existing system. Takes an assertive approach to dealing with existing wrongs, but is not hostile to society nor is a "cop-out." Involves handling any "isms" (e.g., racism, sexism).

- **NONTRADITIONAL KNOWLEDGE ACQUIRED:** Acquires knowledge in a sustained and/or culturally related ways in any area, including social, personal, or interpersonal.

LESSON

From the time you were little boys and girls, whether it was in school, home or another locale, you have probably been told to mind your manners. What the person telling you this meant is that they wanted you to behave properly for the situation in which you were involved or about to be involved. Having and using proper manners is one of the six skills you need to master in life.

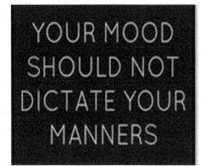

Making a good first impression is essential in many social and business situations. So, learn the proper way to shake hands. This gives you the opportunity to establish your friendliness and accessibility, whether you are greeting your neighbors or starting a new job. Practice your handshake with friends or family members before you start shaking the hands of strangers. Remember that people often initially judge you by your handshake! So, make sure it shows your confidence and pleasant personality.

In life, it is always important to make a good first impression. To do so you must know and practice good manners and proper etiquette.

You only have one chance to make a First Impression!

A first impression can generate one of the statements below.

• I like her/him	• He's/She's a happy person
• She's/He's mean	• He/She always appears to be angry
• Why is she/he so angry	• I don't like to see him/her coming
• She/he has a nice personality	• I really enjoyed meeting him/her
• I like being around her/him	

Handshake

A short ritual in which two people grasp one of each other's right hands, in most cases accompanied by a brief up and down movement of the grasped hands. Using the right hand is generally considered proper etiquette. Customs surrounding handshakes are specific to cultures.

When	How
Initial introduction	Extend your hand for a firm handshake
Job interviews	Make eye contact with others
Professional setting	Use proper speech for each setting
Greeting strangers as host/hostess	Address others with an appropriate greeting
At the opening and/or close of a meeting	Respect other's personal space
Greeting new acquaintance	Reserve gestures and personal movement
Formal settings	Greet others with a pleasant demeanor

FIVE ELEMENTS OF THE HANDSHAKE

APPROACH - If sitting, stand before extending your hand. This shows respect and puts you on the same level as the other person. If you are walking, try to stop, turn, and face the other person, unless it creates an awkward situation.

EYE CONTACT - Make eye contact and a sincere smile and show that you are happy to be where you are. Give your undivided attention to the individual to prevent giving the impression that you are in a hurry.

FIRM GRIP - Give a good, solid, firm grip but not overpowering. Do not give a limp grip. It gives the impression of weakness. However, do not crush the other person's hand. Shake hands in an up-and-down motion.

GREETING - Your greeting should include his or her name and a pleasantry, such as, "It's so nice to meet you, Ms. Jones." If you have more nice things to say, include them at this time, but don't go overboard.

RELEASE - Handshake should only last approximately two to five seconds. Be observant and follow the lead of the other person.

FOOD FOR THOUGHT

THE RIGHT THINGS TO SAY

Sir	Ma'am	May I assist you
Thank you	You are welcome	Yes/No
Please	May I	Allow me
I apologize/I'm sorry	Is it my turn	Hello
Excuse me	My pleasure	Good to see you
Pardon me	I beg your pardon	Nice to meet you
It's your turn	After you	I enjoyed your company

WHAT YOU SHOULD KNOW

Definition of MANNERS

Why it is important to make a good first impression

Why manners are crucial in making a good first impression

ACTIVITY: 3.1 MANNERS

Name:	Date:

Putting it to Practice:

Using the guidelines for proper manners and etiquette describe how you would respond to the situations listed below. Read each scenario and then write your response. Take time to evaluate each response and discuss what you did well and what you can improve upon.

Ask for help from your caring adult he/she can serve as a partner in acting out these scenarios.

Remember to review tips for making a proper first impression when meeting and greeting others in social or professional situations.

Scenario 1: You just bumped into someone by accident while walking through the mall talking to some friends. What would be your response?

Response 1:

Scenario 2: You are waiting on the city bus and left your watch at home. It seems to you that the bus may be running late. How would you ask the person sitting on a nearby bench what time is it?

Response 2:

Scenario 3: You are in a crowd trying to make it to the correct gate to enter the basketball arena. You need to move past several people in a tight situation. How do you address people in order to move through the crowd?

Response 3:

Scenario 4: You are greeting a person at the beginning of an interview for a summer job. What is your initial greeting to this person?

Response 4:

Which of the impressions listed below do you generate when you meet someone or when people see you coming? Why? Check the responses that apply.

_____ I like her/him

_____ She's/He's mean

_____ Why is she/he so angry

_____ She/He has a nice personality

_____ I like being around her/him

_____ He's/She's a happy person

_____ He/She always appears to be angry

_____ I don't like to see him/her coming

_____ I really enjoyed meeting him/her

Practice daily with people in your life using the new tips you have learned from the manners activities.

3.2 ADAPTABILITY

In this unit, you will explore how to adapt to specific settings in the areas of dress, speech and behavior. Different situations and settings require different behaviors. You have to know what behaviors are best given the setting/situation in order to be able to best adapt. All behaviors are not acceptable for all settings.

NONCOGNITIVE VARIABLE(S)

- **REALISTIC SELF-APPRAISAL:** Recognizes and accepts any strengths and deficiencies, especially academic, and works hard at self-development. Recognizes need to broaden individuality.

- **UNDERSTANDS AND KNOWS HOW TO HANDLE THE SYSTEM:** Exhibits a realistic view of the system based upon personal experiences and is committed to improving the existing system. Takes an assertive approach to dealing with existing wrongs, but is not hostile to society nor is a "cop-out." Involves handling any "isms" (e.g., racism, sexism).

- **NONTRADITIONAL KNOWLEDGE ACQUIRED:** Acquires knowledge in a sustained and/or culturally related ways in any area, including social, personal, or interpersonal.

LESSON

You too have to learn to be chameleon-like in life. You have to assess the environment you will be in and be able to determine the proper dress, speech and behavior that is needed for that situation. Then you have to become a master at adapting as needed to any given environment.

Let's consider a very interesting animal called the chameleon. To the left you can see a picture of a chameleon. The unique quality of the chameleon is that it can change colors to blend in to its surroundings. It uses this quality as a defense mechanism to help camouflage itself from predators so it does not stand out and easily fits into the environment. This special quality allows the chameleon to adjust, change and adapt to various difficult situations. The chameleon has to assess surroundings, understand what changes need to be made to blend in, and adapt accordingly.

There are three spaces you must immediately master when using your chameleon-like ability of adapting to the environment. The three spaces are; **Dress, Speech, and Behavior**. Furthermore, there are four zones that will clearly define how you should respond in each situation. In most cases the zones will align perfectly with each other. The zones are **Formal, Semi-formal, Casual, and Informal.** In most situations, the dress code will dictate how to engage in that zone.

DRESS

Formal – ceremonious attire (prom wear, tuxedo, gown, black tie, ceremonial)
Professional/Semi-formal – similar to formal (dark suit, tie, cocktail dress, dressy suit)
Casual – appropriate for informal occasions; not dressy (slacks/shirt, no jeans)
Informal – normally worn relaxing (jeans, sporty wear, jogging suit, never PJs)

SPEECH

Formal – proper language, conversations relative to environment
Professional/Semi-formal – good language
Casual – relaxed nature
Informal – casual, with friends

BEHAVIOR

Formal – act according to the way you are dressed
Professional/Semi-formal – act according to the way you are dressed
Casual – act according to the way you are dressed
Informal – act according to the way you are dressed

Perfecting your chameleon skills:

In order to be ready for adulthood, you have to learn to adapt to the different settings you will be in. Always evaluate every situation to determine its space and the appropriate zone required. As you mature, you will know what to wear, say and do at the appropriate time.

When in doubt, a phone call to your caring adult can help.

FOOD FOR THOUGHT

All of us experience change in our lives.

Change is the one constant in our lives.

There are changes that we look forward to and change that we fear.

However, one thing is for sure:

Things will not stay the same no matter how much we would like them to.

When a life change occurs, we have two choices in how to respond.

We can despair that a change has come and assume that things will be worse,

or we can look with excitement at the new possibilities that the change presents.

WHAT YOU SHOULD KNOW

Understand the parallel between chameleons and change

The three areas to be considered when adapting to various situations

Difference between proper and improper dress, speech and behavior for a given situation

ACTIVITY: 3.2 ADAPTABILITY

Name:	Date:

FORMAL

PROFESSIONAL/SEMI-FORMAL

CASUAL

INFORMAL

Chameleon-like behavior!

What is the most unique quality of a chameleon?

When does a chameleon use this quality?

Why is this quality so special?

Describe how you would dress, speak, and behave in the situations or settings below. In each one of the columns next to each setting listed below, indicate the appropriate zones for each space. With your *Faces of Change 2* caring adult, in the additional spaces provided list some other settings and the appropriate zone. Discuss your responses with that adult, if possible.

Example: If you were meeting friends for dinner, you would probably not dress, speak or behave the same as if you were meeting your boss or co-workers for lunch.

SETTING	DRESS	SPEECH	BEHAVIOR
1. Mall with friends			
2. Job interview			
3. Applying for a job			
4. College tour			
5. Banquet/Dinner			
6. School			
7.			
8.			
9.			
10.			
11.			
12.			
13.			

3.3 SMARTS: DECISION MAKING PROCESS

In this unit, you will work through the decision-making process in order to become familiar with the steps to use when making a decision. In some cases, you will make a decision in a split second or you will have some time to make the decision. Regardless of the amount of time it takes you to make the decision, the process for making the decision is the same. Request your caring adult assistance with the steps as you work through how to properly make a decision.

NONCOGNITIVE VARIABLE(S)

- **REALISTIC SELF-APPRAISAL:** Recognizes and accepts any strengths and deficiencies, especially academic, and works hard at self-development. Recognizes need to broaden individuality.

- **UNDERSTANDS AND KNOWS HOW TO HANDLE THE SYSTEM:** Exhibits a realistic view of the system based upon personal experiences and is committed to improving the existing system. Takes an assertive approach to dealing with existing wrongs, but is not hostile to society nor is a "cop-out." Involves handling any "isms" (e.g., racism, sexism).

- **NONTRADITIONAL KNOWLEDGE ACQUIRED:** Acquires knowledge in a sustained and/or culturally related ways in any area, including social, personal, or interpersonal.

LESSON

Regardless of how smart you are, you must master the art of decision making. You make decisions every day. What will you eat? How will you spend your time? Where will you go? In doing so, you are engaging in a decision-making process. Making good, positive choices is essential in adulthood. It is the third skill you must MASTER.

"By the way, intelligence to me isn't just being book-smart or having a college degree; it's trusting your gut instincts, being intuitive, thinking outside the box, and sometimes just realizing that things need to change and being smart enough to change it."

Tabatha Coffey

"Half of being smart is knowing what you are dumb about."

Solomon Short

Most people, if asked, would say they consider themselves to be a smart, intelligent person. The question isn't so much are you smart, but what kind of smart are you?

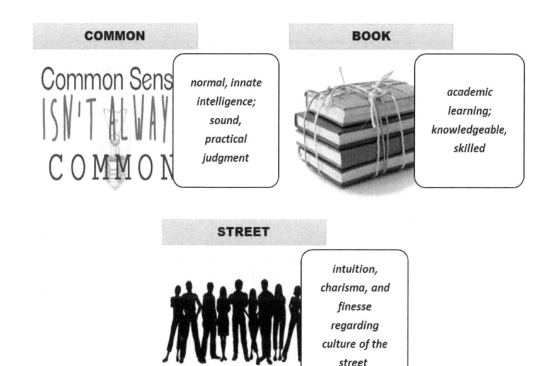

COMMON	BOOK
normal, innate intelligence; sound, practical judgment	academic learning; knowledgeable, skilled

STREET

intuition, charisma, and finesse regarding culture of the street

After reviewing the scenarios below, then make a choice regarding the decision most appropriate for you to achieve your desired results.

Think about what you learned after implementing your choice. Review the outcome so you will have a reference point when addressing similar issues/situations in the future.

The key is to learn to make decisions which produce positive results instead of negative consequences. Keep in mind some decisions you make can last a lifetime!

Decision Making Process

STEP 1: **ISSUE/SITUATION**	Clearly identify the issue/situation you are facing that requires action. Make it definitive based on your interpretation. Issue example: Lose weight
STEP 2: **OPTIONS/ACTION**	Consider what options are available for issue/situation. Identifying options can be done two different ways: one is based on your previous experience; the other is witnessing or knowledge of how someone else dealt with this same issue. 1. Diet 2. Exercise/Workout 3. Combination of both 1 & 2
STEP 3: **PLAN**	Each option will require a different resolution plan. Always consider your expected outcomes when creating your plans. 1. Type of diet (vegetarian, protein, what's best for me to eat, etc.) 2. Type of workout (when, where, how long, cost, equipment needed, etc.) 3. Combination of both
STEP 4: **CHOICE/ DECISION**	Make a decision on which choice works best for you to achieve your desired results. Look at three things: the issue/situation, your options/actions and your plans. After reviewing all three, decide which is most appropriate for you. Making the choice also requires that you immediately implement your actions and plans. Choice 1 - works best for me Choice 2 - works best for me Choice 3 - works best for me

STEP 5: **REFLECTION/CONSEQUENCE**	Every decision has a consequence. Consequences may be positive or negative, reversible or irreversible. Hence, it is crucial that you always weigh the consequences of your decisions before you act.			

	P - Positive a good, affirmative, or constructive quality or attribute.	**N- Negative** not desirable or optimistic.	**R –** **Reversible** able to be turned the other way around.	**I – Irreversible** not able to be undone or altered.

FOOD FOR THOUGHT

Hard Choices

A path is laid out ahead,

it forks before your feet.

A decision filled with dread,

uncertain of what you'll meet.

A game full of chance,

of many hidden pit falls.

To find true romance,

dare you risk losing all?

Choices never easy to make,

fog seems to cloud your way.

You fear making a mistake,

of gambling and losing the day.

But life is full of Hard Choices,

and risk is part of the game.

Be brave, ignore doubting voices,

make the choice, life won't be the same.

Jojoba Mansell

"A lesson learned is not a lesson learned until it is applied and changes human behavior!"

Colonel (retired) Sammie Hargrove

WHAT YOU SHOULD KNOW

Making a decision is a process

The five steps of the decision-making process

Explain why making good decisions is important in life

ACTIVITY: 3.3 SMARTS: DECISION MAKING PROCESS

Name:	Date:

Decision Making Process Worksheet

Making good, positive choices is essential in adulthood. The more you execute the decision-making process, the easier these steps will become.   Let's practice the decision-making process. Use the steps in the lesson as your guide.

ISSUE/SITUATION Examples: Study more, Smoking, Dropout, etc.

COLUMN 1 ISSUE/SITUATION	COLUMN 2 OPTIONS/ACTIONS	COLUMN 3 PLAN	COLUMN 4 CHOICE/DECISION	COLUMN 5 REFLECTION/ CONSEQUENCE			
1.	A.	A.	A.	P	N	R	I
	B.	B.	B.	P	N	R	I
	C.	C.	C.	P	N	R	I
	D.	D	D.	P	N	R	I
2.	A.	A.	A.	P	N	R	I
	B.	B.	B.	P	N	R	I
	C.	C.	C.	P	N	R	I
	D.	D.	D.	P	N	R	I
3.	A.	A.	A.	P	N	R	I
	B.	B.	B.	P	N	R	I
	C.	C.	C.	P	N	R	I
	D.	D.	D.	P	N	R	I

3.4 TRUSTWORTHY

So far you have been looking at skills that you must master in life to transition into a productive, successful adult. You are now about to explore an important trait that is needed if you want to be successful. This trait requires you to work hard and master in much the same way you approach the three M.A.S.T.E.R skills we have covered so far.

NONCOGNITIVE VARIABLE(S)

- **REALISTIC SELF-APPRAISAL:** Recognizes and accepts any strengths and deficiencies, especially academic, and works hard at self-development. Recognizes need to broaden individuality.

- **UNDERSTANDS AND KNOWS HOW TO HANDLE THE SYSTEM:** Exhibits a realistic view of the system based upon personal experiences and is committed to improving the existing system. Takes an assertive approach to dealing with existing wrongs, but is not hostile to society nor is a "cop-out." Involves handling any "isms" (e.g., racism, sexism).

- **POSITIVE SELF-CONCEPT:** Demonstrates confidence, strength of character, determination, and independence.

LESSON

TRUST IS LIKE A PIECE OF PAPER. ONCE IT'S CRUMPLED, IT CAN'T BE PERFECT AGAIN.

What does it mean to be "TRUSTWORTHY"?	trait of trusting; of believing in the honesty and reliability of others; "the experience destroyed his trust and personal dignity"
	certainty based on past experience; "he wrote the paper with considerable reliance on the work of other scientists"
As you work to define trustworthy let's explore it's root word, "TRUST":	complete confidence in a person or plan etc.; "he cherished the faith of a good woman"; "the doctor-patient relationship is based on trust"
	a trustful relationship; "he took me into his confidence"; "he betrayed their trust"
	be confident about something; "I believe that he will come back from the war"
	expect with desire; "I trust you will behave better from now on"; "I hope she understands that she cannot expect a raise"
	extend credit to; to confer a trust upon; "The messenger was entrusted with the general's secret"

Trustworthy:

Always do what you say and say what you mean – honor your commitments and be honest in all aspects of life

Always do your best – never cut corners or try to get by with the minimum

Always make sure to stay above reproach; behave and live in such a way that others see you as being better than average

FOOD FOR THOUGHT

Trust

It's so simple, so basic,
Yet we lack it.
Interaction is nothing without it.
Unable to make a bond because the fact is,
We've missed the point.
The point that connects you and me,
And not just on a family tree;
That connects us all from A to Z,
And not just on eHarmony.
Trust.

Where did it go?
Or did we even have it years ago?
Afraid to go on the right track,
Because we might get stabbed in the back.

Locking our doors and checking it twice,
Like we're Santa Clause on a Christmas
blight.
Putting a lock on our phone for protection,
Because your friends may use it as a weapon.
Hiding what belongs to us,
Because we lost our trust in all our lust.
But trusting each other is a must,
Because you can't spell trust without us.
Trust.

A firm belief in the reliability,
Truth, Ability, or Strength in someone.
Can you think of anyone?
I am sure you can,
Maybe the one that holds your hand.
But for how long?
I'm sorry but it's true,
People can back-stab you.
But this can change starting with you,
Because if you trust people,
They'll trust you.
You may get hurt but at least you'll live,
With your heart on your sleeve and
something to give.

So, let's break this cycle of deceit and start
this world anew.
It doesn't start with them, it starts with you.
Trust someone and you will see,
How great this world could be,
for you and me.
It's not that hard so don't make it be,
It's only the fear of the possibility,
Of losing everything.
Don't fear,
Trust.

Anonymous

WHAT YOU SHOULD KNOW

Definition of trustworthiness

How to demonstrate trustworthiness

Explain why it is important to be considered trustworthy

ACTIVITY: 3.4 TRUSTWORTHY

Name:	Date:

What Would You Do?

Trustworthiness is being dependable, responsible, and credible. In the following scenarios, what would you do to demonstrate your trustworthiness?

Scenario 1:
Your parent(s)/guardian(s) have to leave for work before you and your siblings leave for school. They have given you specific instructions to follow each day for dressing and feeding your siblings, getting them to the bus, and making sure the house is secure before you leave for school. Part of their instructions include not allowing anyone in the house. Since it is a cold morning, some of your friends come over to ask if they can wait inside with you since your house is closer to the bus stop. What would you do?

Scenario 2:
On Thursdays after school, you have been helping an older couple in the neighborhood with some chores around the house. Sometimes they pay you for your help. Almost every time you are there they offer you a meal. It is Thursday. At lunch, everyone is excited about the game this afternoon with the school's rival. Everyone is going and anticipate a big celebration after the game if your school's team wins. They ask you to go this week. What would you do? Why? What thoughts would you have in deciding what to do?

Scenario 3:
Have you ever been faced with a situation where you were at a crossroad regarding being honest or dishonest? What if you could be dishonest and no one would ever find out? What would you do? Describe how you would handle the situation. What decision would you make? Why? How did you go about making the decision?

3.5 EXCELLENCE

In this unit, you will re-define homework as self-work and complete the Strength, Weakness, Opportunity, and Threat (S.W.O.T.) analysis of yourself. You will examine what it means to go the extra mile and strive for excellence in all areas of life.

NONCOGNITIVE VARIABLE(S)

- **REALISTIC SELF-APPRAISAL:** Recognizes and accepts any strengths and deficiencies, especially academic, and works hard at self-development. Recognizes need to broaden individuality.

- **UNDERSTANDS AND KNOWS HOW TO HANDLE THE SYSTEM:** Exhibits a realistic view of the system based upon personal experiences and is committed to improving the existing system. Takes an assertive approach to dealing with existing wrongs, but is not hostile to society nor is a "cop-out." Involves handling any "isms" (e.g., racism, sexism).

- **NONTRADITIONAL KNOWLEDGE ACQUIRED:** Acquires knowledge in a sustained and/or culturally related ways in any area, including social, personal, or interpersonal.

LESSON

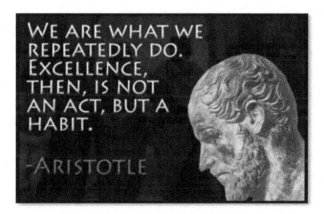

If you visit any book store, take notice that the largest unit of the store is the self-help section. The books and materials in this area include leadership skills, nutrition and wellness. Why are there more books in this section? It's because most of us, at some point in life, have a desire to improve. You cannot simply will yourself to make progress. There must be strategies and tactics to reach your improvement goals. Now you have to begin to move from where you are now toward progression; keeping in mind that you want to be a successful adult.

FOOD FOR THOUGHT

Going the Extra Mile

In the ancient Roman Empire if you were a slave and you met a Roman soldier while traveling, that soldier had the right to ask you to carry his property for a mile. You did not have to be his servant; you could belong to anyone and still have to fulfill this duty. Did you know that the phrase "going the extra mile" came from this practice? A slave was only required to go one mile with the soldier. Doing anything more would be going over and above what was required. Part of mastering yourself is learning to "go the extra mile," doing more than what is required or expected. This is excellence defined; doing more than is required or expected of you at all times and in all areas of life.

It is not easy to always go the extra mile. It is much easier to just do what it takes to get it done. In order to master yourself, you must be willing to work at everything. This is the best way to cultivate and grow excellence. Excellence should be the goal for every aspect of your life. Others will notice this trait in you and you will have a sense of achievement and earn respect.

WHAT YOU SHOULD KNOW

Definition of excellence

What it means to go the extra mile (achieve excellence) in various aspects of life?

Understand how to cultivate excellence in your life?

ACTIVITY: 3.5 EXCELLENCE

Name:	Date:

In the areas below, record how you can you improve and move closer to achieving your goals with excellence? Complete the assessment chart.

CATEGORIES	C - Effort Average	B - Effort Above Average	A – Effort Extra Mile
Grades			
Chores at home			
Attendance at school			
Academic			
Behavior, conduct			
Attitude			

3.5.1 EXCELLENCE – WEAKNESSES TO STRENGTHS

In this unit, you will create and execute a plan to convert your weaknesses into strengths.

NONCOGNITIVE VARIABLE(S)

- **REALISTIC SELF-APPRAISAL:** Recognizes and accepts any strengths and deficiencies, especially academic, and works hard at self-development. Recognizes need to broaden individuality.

- **UNDERSTANDS AND KNOWS HOW TO HANDLE THE SYSTEM:** Exhibits a realistic view of the system based upon personal experiences and is committed to improving the existing system. Takes an assertive approach to dealing with existing wrongs, but is not hostile to society nor is a "cop-out." Involves handling any "isms" (e.g., racism, sexism).

- **NONTRADITIONAL KNOWLEDGE ACQUIRED:** Acquires knowledge in a sustained and/or culturally related ways in any area, including social, personal, or interpersonal.

LESSON

Weakness to Strength Planning:

You have already started the process of completing a personal S.W.O.T analysis. Furthermore, you have identified several of your weaknesses. Now that you have those weaknesses identified, time to begin transforming those weaknesses into strengths. The goal is excellence and you must be willing to develop an improvement plan and work that plan. Take a moment to look back at your S.W.O.T chart, especially those weaknesses you listed.

- Where can you improve?
- What should you avoid?
- What do others see as your weaknesses?
- What areas present challengers?

If you are truly working your plan, you will probably have little trouble avoiding those threats you listed on your S.W.O.T. chart. It is important to recognize what threats may distract you. Maintaining your focus and working your plan helps eliminate threats. The best defense from threats is awareness and preparation. Prepare for excellence and success will follow.

The process of converting your weaknesses to strengths must always be intentional.

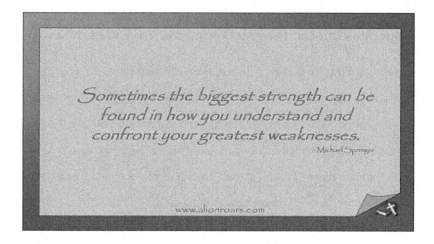

Again, consider this from an internal and external basis. Do other people see **WEAKNESSES** that you don't see? It's best to be as realistic as possible and face any unpleasant truths as soon as possible.

STRENGTHS/OPPORTUNITIES	STRENGTHS/THREATS
How can you use your strengths to take advantage of your opportunities? Consider all strengths listed in the S.W.O.T. one by one. Analyze each opportunity to determine how each internal strength can help you capitalize on each external opportunity.	How can you use your strengths to avoid real and potential threats? Consider all strengths listed in the S.W.O.T. one by one. Analyze each threat to determine how each internal strength can help you avoid every external threat.
WEAKNESSES/OPPORTUNITIES	**WEAKNESSES/THREATS**
How can you use your opportunities to overcome weaknesses you have been experiencing? Consider all weaknesses listed in the S.W.O.T. one by one. Analyze each opportunity to determine how each internal weakness can be eliminated by using each external opportunity.	How can you minimize weaknesses and avoid threats? Consider all weaknesses listed in the S.W.O.T. one by one. Analyze each threat to determine how both can be avoided.

FOOD FOR THOUGHT

Success in Life, How to Overcome Your Weaknesses

In your journey to success, you will encounter weaknesses in your life.

If you don't deal with them, they will hinder you or stop you altogether from reaching success.

Having weaknesses isn't really the big deal because we all have them.

If you don't overcome those weaknesses that's when you are in trouble.

Here are three keys you can use to overcome your weaknesses.

Learn how to improve it.

Surround yourself with people's strengths.

Learn from others.

Jason Osborn

WHAT YOU SHOULD KNOW

Recognize and acknowledge your weaknesses

Identify opportunities for improving weaknesses

Understand how not addressing weaknesses and ignoring threats can obstruct progress toward excellence

ACTIVITY: 3.5.1 EXCELLENCE – WEAKNESSES TO STRENGTHS

Name:	Date:

WEAKNESSES Insert the weakness you identified during your S.W.O.T. analysis: one per column on line labeled WEAKNESSES. Prioritize each weakness based on what you feel you need to work on immediately.	1.	2.
OPPORTUNITIES On this row, list all resources available to assist with improving or removing this particular weakness. List has no minimum or maximum number. Include any and all resources you can think of. Your caring adult can be a big help in helping you build this list. Resources can be programs, people, books, websites, etc.	1. 2. 3. 4. 5.	1. 2. 3. 4. 5.
CRITICAL DATES On this row, pinpoint dates which resources are available to assist you in working on weakness.	1. 2. 3. 4.	1. 2. 3. 4.
THREATS On this row, list possible obstacles that could occur if you do not improve or remove that weakness.	1. 2. 3. 4.	1. 2. 3. 4.

3.6 RESPECT

In this unit, you will examine the concept of respect by considering how and why you should respect yourself and others.

NONCOGNITIVE VARIABLE(S)

- **REALISTIC SELF-APPRAISAL:** Recognizes and accepts any strengths and deficiencies, especially academic, and works hard at self-development. Recognizes need to broaden individuality.

- **UNDERSTANDS AND KNOWS HOW TO HANDLE THE SYSTEM:** Exhibits a realistic view of the system based upon personal experiences and is committed to improving the existing system. Takes an assertive approach to dealing with existing wrongs, but is not hostile to society nor is a "cop-out." Involves handling any "isms" (e.g., racism, sexism).

- **NONTRADITIONAL KNOWLEDGE ACQUIRED:** Acquires knowledge in a sustained and/or culturally related ways in any area, including social, personal, or interpersonal.

LESSON

The last skill that you have to acquire to complete the MASTER process is Respect. The act of respecting yourself and others is the guiding principle in interactions with others, especially with those who may not look like or think like you do. All successful adults know what it means to respect self and others.

Respect for self and those around you are the driving force for actions and interactions in life. Mutual respect should be the foundation of all the relationships you have. How you care for and treat yourself and others speaks volumes about you. Make sure when interacting with other people that you observe how others interact. These two actions will help you remember to show respect.

Being able to respect others can be challenging. You can show respect for others by:

- acknowledging everyone's worth
- making it a point to look at others and listen while they are talking
- recognizing all people are of equal worth
- showing gestures of kindness
- practicing the manners learned in previous unit
- being thoughtful concerning the feelings and preferences of others
- willing to serve and not always have to be served
- willing to give and not always have to receive

FOOD FOR THOUGHT

Awesome Respect Quotes

Jackie Robinson — *"I'm not concerned with your liking or disliking me... All I ask is that you respect me as a human being."*

Henri Frederic Amiel — *"There is no respect for others without humility in one's self."*

Albert Einstein — *"Everyone should be respected as an individual, but no one idolized."*

Dr. Seuss — *"A person's a person no matter how small."*

Muhammad Ali — *"Hating people because of their color is wrong. And it doesn't matter which color does the hating. It's just plain wrong."*

Bryant H. McGill — *"One of the sincerest forms of respect is actually listening to what another has to say."*

Stephen Covey — *"Moral authority comes from following universal and timeless principles like honesty, integrity, treating people with respect."*

Nash Grier — *"I accept you, and you get the same respect from me whether you are black, white, gay straight, Asian, bisexual, Australian, tall, fat, whatever it is. We are all people, and I look at the people of the world the same way, as my brothers and sisters."*

Paul Watson — *"Sometimes we are separated by differences, and sometimes we are united by common ideals of respect and compassion."*

Dr. Martin Luther King Jr. — *"People fail to get along because they fear each other; they fear each other because they don't know each other; they don't know each other because they have not communicated with each other."*

WHAT YOU SHOULD KNOW

Definition of respect

How to respect yourself

How to show respect for others

ACTIVITY: 3.6 RESPECT

Name:	Date:

What Is Your Story?

Having respect for yourself and others is a trait that all people must work to obtain. Respect for self and those around you is the driving force for actions and interactions in life. Mutual respect should be the foundation of all the relationships you have.

Take a Look in the Mirror

Being able to respect yourself can be challenging. As previously stated, you have to be able to look at yourself in the mirror, see yourself as you really are, and like what you see.

When you look in the mirror, what do you see about yourself that you like?

Can others see that you respect yourself? How?

How do you carry yourself and what do you do that says you respect who you are? (e.g. I make sure I am well-groomed when I am in public.)

Take a Look Around

Can others see your respect for them? How?

What are some ways you show respect for others?

4.0 EXPANDING YOUR COMFORT ZONE – WARM UP

We live in a global world where we are in daily contact with people who are not like us. For some people this is uncomfortable and awkward because they are so accustomed to living in their own circles with little or no interaction with those who may be different. To successfully transition into adulthood, you must be able to interact with others regardless of your differences. You have to be willing to expand your borders. Being well-equipped for the adult world requires the ability and willingness to move out of one's own world. Youth must be able to interact with and understand others who may not hold the same beliefs, behave in the same way, or look the same as they do. This unit takes a look at how and why we have zones of comfort in which we tend to live. More importantly, it helps youth begin to think outside of that comfort zone so that they are ready to interact with everyone they may come in contact with in the adult world.

NONCOGNITIVE VARIABLE(S)

- **POSITIVE SELF-CONCEPT:** Demonstrates confidence, strength of character, determination, and independence.

- **REALISTIC SELF-APPRAISAL:** Recognizes and accepts any strengths and deficiencies, especially academic, and works hard at self-development. Recognizes need to broaden individuality.

- **NONTRADITIONAL KNOWLEDGE ACQUIRED:** Acquires knowledge in a sustained and/or culturally related ways in any area, including social, personal, or interpersonal.

LESSON

"You cannot fully understand your

Own life without knowing or thinking

Beyond your life, your own neighborhood,

And even your own nation."

Johnetta Cole

"You have to leave the city of comfort

And go into the wilderness of your intuition.

What you will discover will be wonderful.

what you will discover is yourself.

Alan Alda

While you must be prepared to transition into adulthood with skill development and mastery over time. Becoming an adult in today's society means being able to function both within your own culture and in others as well. Our increasingly global world mandates that we are prepared to work and live with others. Diversity is our present and our future. To be successful, you must be able to transcend your own comfort zones and interact with others who may not look, think, behave, or have the same beliefs. Being well-equipped for the adult world requires the ability and willingness to move out of your own world and allows you to move into a successful, productive adulthood.

In this unit, you will:

- Recognize you have comfort zones in which you live and operate
- Identify your comfort zones
- Recognize how comfort zones are created
- Explore how to expand your comfort zones
- Explore and evaluate new zones
- Identify and avoid danger zones
- Understand the importance of being able to operate outside of your own comfort zones
- Learn how to code switch

Most of us have been in situations where we were uncomfortable and didn't quite feel at ease! We have all probably had a time when we felt out of place. As you transition into adulthood, it is very important for you to recognize when you are and are not comfortable in a particular situation and why. This way you can begin to learn how to cope with and behave properly in all types of situations.

FOOD FOR THOUGHT

My Comfort Zone

I used to have a comfort zone
where I knew I couldn't fail,
The same four walls of busy work
were really more like a jail

I longed so much to do the things
I'd never done before,
But I stayed inside my comfort zone
and paced the same old floor

I said it didn't matter
that I wasn't doing much,
I said I didn't care for things
like diamonds or furs and such

I claimed to be so busy
with the things inside my zone,
But deep inside I longed for
something special of my own

I couldn't let my life go by
just watching others win,
I held my breath and stepped outside
to let the change begin

I took a step and with new strength
I'd never felt before,
I kissed my comfort zone good bye
and closed and locked the door

If you are in a comfort zone
afraid to venture out,
Remember that all winners
were at one time filled with doubt

A step or two and words of praise
can make your dreams come true
Greet your future with a smile,
success is there for you!

Anonymous

WHAT YOU SHOULD KNOW

Understand you live in a global world

Recognize the need to be able to interact with others in a global manner

Explain what makes you uncomfortable about new, different situations

ACTIVITY: 4.0 EXPANDING YOUR COMFORT ZONE – WARM UP

Name:	Date:

- How would you feel, act or behave in each setting presented in the activity below?
- Why you would feel/behave that way?
- What would make you comfortable or uncomfortable about the situation?

Picture Yourself....

 **Picture 1:** In a business office where everyone is dressed in professional attire and you are dressed casual. (example: I would feel uncomfortable and out of place if the people were dressed differently than me.)

 **Picture 2:** At a music concert with your friends and one of your favorite artist.

 **Picture 3:** In a fancy restaurant in the city where there were white tablecloths and formal table settings.

 **Picture 4:** At the mall in an upscale store where you don't normally shop.

 **Picture 5:** At a formal reception or social gathering, such as a wedding, prom, or banquet.

4.1 IN A ZONE AND DANGER ZONE

In this unit, you will explore the concept of comfort zones and learn to recognize the zones of comfort in your own life. You will look at why we all are creatures of habit, forming zones of comfort in which we live and operate. You will begin to identify some of your specific zones of comfort.

NONCOGNITIVE VARIABLE(S)

- **REALISTIC SELF-APPRAISAL:** Recognizes and accepts any strengths and deficiencies, especially academic, and works hard at self-development. Recognizes need to broaden individuality.

- **UNDERSTANDS AND KNOWS HOW TO HANDLE THE SYSTEM:** Exhibits a realistic view of the system based upon personal experiences and is committed to improving the existing system. Takes an assertive approach to dealing with existing wrongs, but is not hostile to society nor is a "cop-out." Involves handling any "isms" (e.g., racism, sexism).

LESSON

Creatures of Comfort

For most of us, our culture and experiences shape our comfort zones. Culture is defined as the beliefs and behavior patterns of a group of people that are gained through social learning and passed down to others in the group. Your culture is what you learn directly and indirectly as you transition through the phases of life. We are creatures of comfort; what we learn and what we are exposed to often tends to determine what we do later in life.

What is a COMFORT ZONE?

A comfort zone is the circle of interaction and influence possessed by a particular person or group of people. It is characterized by the beliefs and codes of behavior that typify an individual person or the members of a particular group.

Your culture tends to shape your comfort zone. The level of education you aspire to have, the sports you play and enjoy, and music you listen to are all influences and shape your culture.

Sports, education, and music are a few zones of comfort. There are many others zones of comfort as well. You have comfort zones that you may not have realized were comfort zones because most they are second nature because of your culture. It is very easy to be operating in a particular zone your whole life and not realize that you are doing so.

Sports

Athletes tend to associate with other athletes with common interests. The thought patterns, beliefs, and actions of one athlete can affect those of another because they are in the same zone of interaction and influence. They tend to have similar life experiences, so they have a level of comfort with one another because they can identify with the other person.

Education

People of a particular level of education tend to surround themselves with others with that same level of education. The standard of living, economic power, beliefs, thought patterns, and types of decisions can differ greatly from those of someone from another educational level.

Music

The types of music you listen to can be a comfort zone. You may not make the effort to spend time listening to other types of music. Therefore, you might not feel comfortable listening to different genres.

Congratulations, you have just learned to recognize zones of comfort in your own lives. Having our likes and tendencies to migrate towards what we like and what is comfortable is not a bad practice. However, it can become a dangerous practice when we are so in tune with our preferences that we are unable or unwilling to reach outside of them towards others.

What is a DANGER ZONE?

A danger zone is any zone with codes of behavior or patterns of thought that involve illegal or unethical activities or behaviors that could cause harm to yourself and others, physically or otherwise.

Uneasiness and discomfort are to be expected when you try something new, especially expanding your zone. It is important to be able to identify danger zones when you are observing and exploring new zones of comfort.

No comfort zone or code of behavior that characterizes that comfort zone is better than any other unless it involves illegal or unethical activities; they are just different. Be careful not to rank comfort zones by placing one above another. Remember, there are appropriate codes for appropriate situations. The key is recognizing a zone and knowing when to switch your code of behavior.

FOOD FOR THOUGHT

10 Ways to Step Out of Your Comfort Zone and Into Greatness

1. FACE A FEAR THAT YOU HAVE

- Do you have a fear that's been hanging around awhile? Does it come to mind and then goes dormant for lack of pushing yourself? Many people fear public speaking. Maybe it's asking for a raise, or forgiving someone who has hurt you. Think of that one fear that may be holding you back from your potential and set a goal to tackle it in the next three months. When you overcome that fear, reward yourself for your victory and for improving yourself.

2. DO WHAT SCARES YOU EVERY DAY

- Eleanor Roosevelt said, "Do one thing every day that scares you." How powerful would it be to make a conscious effort to do what scares you? What would open up? New friendships? New opportunities? Start out by making a list of three things at the beginning of the week and challenge yourself to do each one during the week. Make it fun and see what good things transpire.

3. MAKE A BOLD MOVE TOWARDS A GOAL

- Sometimes you just need to throw your hats over the wall and take a big risk for big rewards. For example, many people dream to leave their corporate jobs to pursue a hobby that has been a passion. They just need to figure out how to make it happen. The first step is to set a SMART: goal, which is specific, measurable, achievable, realistic and time-limited. Following is an example. I will leave my corporate job to pursue a freelance writing career. Make sure the goal is realistic and achievable within the timeframe you set. Then create a plan with action steps. Next take one small action every day towards your goal, or at least once a week. Before long you will have made real progress and feel good about yourself too.

4. CHANGE YOUR MINDSET

- Changing your thoughts can help you move in the right direction. This takes mental stamina and discipline. A helpful way to start retraining your mind is by creating affirmations having to do with what you desire and/or whom you want to become and repeat them every day. Eventually these affirmations will become a part of your belief system.

5. EXPLORE YOUR FEARS

- There are certain general fears that impede progress like the fear of success or the fear of failure. To make progress, you first need to explore and identify what fears may be holding you back. Then you can work to face and resolve them so that you can move ahead with your plans or keep as is.

6. GROW TO YOUR NEXT LEVEL

- What we perceive as negative about ourselves can limit us. Perhaps something happened and then we made a decision not to go down that path again. It takes courage to get beyond pain, step up your game and grow. Author Saji Ijiyemi said, "A lot of people desire to go to their next level but only a few are determined to grow to their next level." To grow to your next level, first find out what this means to you and then be willing to take on the challenge.

7. CHANGE YOUR LOOK

- Our interior world, our thoughts and beliefs are often reflected in our exterior world, which includes our behaviors and physical appearance. For example, you may be struggling with self-confidence and, unknowingly, trying to hide to avoid attention because of your appearance. A makeover can boost your confidence. You can wear different clothing, get a new haircut or lose some weight. It may be uncomfortable at first to make these changes, but you will send a powerful message to your inner-self that you are strong and worthy.

8. HAVE A TOUGH CONVERSATION

- "A person's success in life can usually be measured by the number of uncomfortable conversations he or she is willing to have," says Author Tim Ferris. Having a conversation with a friend, loved one or co-worker about something that bothers you is one of the most difficult and courageous things to do. Also, it is one of the most responsible and effective ways to create deeper connections and build confidence.

9. PRACTICE BELIEVING IN YOURSELF

- Our belief systems or thoughts can paralyze us. If we think negatively about our abilities, then we create ruts. To get out of a rut or bad habit, explore ways that you can practice believing in yourself. Some ways might include creating a vision board of various goals and inspirational messages and/or practice visualization to help manifest your dreams and who you want to be.

10. TRY SOMETHING NEW

- A way to step out of what is familiar is to explore new and different things. You can start by creating a bucket list, which is a list of all the experiences you would like to have in your lifetime like travel, run a marathon, do yoga, write a book, play an instrument, ride on a zip line, become an entrepreneur. This bucket list is a great way to help you think of new ways to step out of your comfort zone.

Source: Virtues for Life, The Heart of Everyday Living

WHAT YOU SHOULD KNOW

Definition of culture

Understand the concept of comfort zones

Recognize zones of comfort in your life

ACTIVITY: 4.1.1 IN A ZONE

Name:	Date:

Creatures of Comfort:

We are creatures of comfort. What we learn and what we are exposed to tends to determine what we do later in life.

Create a list of your personal comfort zones and how they may be hindering you from moving forward and why?

COMFORT ZONE	EXPLAIN WHY?
1.	
2.	
3.	
4.	
5.	
6.	
7.	
8.	
9.	
10.	
11.	
12.	

Your Zones of Comfort:

Take a moment to think about the types of things you feel comfortable and at ease doing. Complete the chart below with what you do for enjoyment in the given categories. Also, stretch your thinking with activities outside of your comfort zone.

CATEGORY	LIKE/STRETCH
1. SPORTS	I like: (example: watch basketball)
	Stretch: (example: watched tennis)
2. ENTERTAINMENT	I like:
	Stretch:
3. MUSIC	I like:
	Stretch:
4. FOOD	I like:
	Stretch:
5. HOBBIES	I like:
	Stretch:
6. LANGUAGE	I like:
	Stretch:
7. PEOPLE	I like:
	Stretch:

ACTIVITY: 4.1.2 DANGER ZONE

Name:	Date:

Uneasiness and discomfort are to be expected when you try something new, especially expanding your zone. It is important to be able to identify danger zones when you are observing and exploring new zones of comfort. A danger zone is any zone with codes of behavior or patterns of thought that involve illegal or unethical activities or behavior that could cause yourself and others hurt or harm, physically or otherwise.

List danger zones or dangerous activities that are unsafe and could cause you harm.

1.

2.

3.

4.

5.

6.

7.

8.

9.

With your caring adult discuss ways you can recognize a danger zone.

Example: Illegal activity or mistreatment of others could alert you to a danger zone.

4.2 COMFORT ZONE ENABLERS

Now that you have explored what some of your comfort zones are, let's look at why we have comfort zones and/or how we continue in these comfort zones in life. In this unit, you will define and identify comfort zone enablers so you can recognize these enablers in your own life. Both you and your caring adult guides will define zone enablers and explore how specific areas in life aid in the creation of zones of comfort.

NONCOGNITIVE VARIABLE(S)

- **POSITIVE SELF-CONCEPT:** Demonstrates confidence, strength of character, determination, and independence.

- **REALISTIC SELF-APPRAISAL:** Recognizes and accepts any strengths and deficiencies, especially academic, and works hard at self-development. Recognizes need to broaden individuality.

- **UNDERSTANDS AND KNOWS HOW TO HANDLE THE SYSTEM:** Exhibits a realistic view of the system based upon personal experiences and is committed to improving the existing system. Takes an assertive approach to dealing with existing wrongs, but is not hostile to society nor is a "cop-out." Involves handling any "isms" (e.g., racism, sexism).

LESSON

It is easy to live and interact with others while still in your zone of comfort. Sometimes it is difficult to see that you are living in your own box, rarely exploring new zones of comfort in your life. It is essential that you learn to be comfortable with other people, places, and ways of thinking in order to be prepared for life as an adult. It is equally important to be able to recognize the types of enablers that cause us to be and stay in a zone.

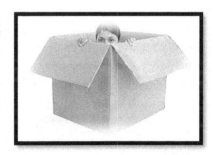

Comfort Zone Enabler is anything that creates or causes the development of a zone of comfort in a person or a group of people. For example, appearance can be a zone enabler in that the way a person appears can put them in a zone of comfort. If you dress a certain way, you will more than likely be associated with a particular group of people who also dress that same way. Your appearance has enabled you to be in a zone of comfort. This allows you to feel safe and at ease with others who share the same comfort zone. Zone Enablers create barriers which unconsciously causes you to stay in your comfort zones. Enablers box you into your zones.

We all have comfort zones which can be difficult to recognize. You have to make a conscious effort to see those enablers in your life when dealing with others so that you can operate outside your comfort zones.

You must learn to reach out to others, even when it makes you uncomfortable. Listed below are several enablers.

Race	Stereotypes	Politics
Gender	Economics	Appearance
Geographic Location	Religion	Neighborhood

FOOD FOR THOUGHT

Leave Your Comfort Zone

"When you feel overwhelmed, just remember that for eagles, too, it's the price of flying!"

The mother eagle makes her nest high on a cliff's edge. So, high, in fact that the baby eagle is literally so terrified of its "free fall" that it will not leave the nest **unless pushed out by its mother! Imagine the** confusion of the baby eagle when its mother, who up to this point has been nurturing and attentive, suddenly seems to turn on him, pushing him from the nest and-forcing him to fly! But, of course, in the end, pushed from the confines of a nest now outgrown, the baby eagle takes flight and learns that everything's going to be okay. Because, you see, in the free fall, the young eagle learns to trust its wings! It's an important lesson: When your challenges seem overwhelming, when you feel frightened or confused, when you're being called to leave behind something familiar but outgrown, remember the baby eagle. You, too, can soar-but first you'll have to leave the safety of your comfort zone! Momentarily "overwhelmed" is to be expected, so don't let it stop you from reaching new heights in your life.

Taste-berry promise for the day: I will not fear the price of learning to "fly"! I will take one positive action that is outside my comfort zone.

Source: Taste-berry Inspiration for Teens

WHAT YOU SHOULD KNOW

Definition of Zone Enabler

Understand how you can become enabled in a zone of comfort

Recognize zone enablers in your interactions with others

ACTIVITY: 4.2 COMFORT ZONE ENABLERS

Name:		Date:

Exploring Zone Enablers: Listed below in the column on the left are some typical zone enabler types, things that can cause divisions among individuals or groups and areas in life around which comfort zones are created. In the space below, write the types of enablers and then in the column to the right of that enabler write a statement regarding how that enabler causes the comfort zone to exist. Discuss how that particular enabler can aid in the creation of a zone of comfort. When giving your answer, consider how these enablers may have caused you to develop your comfort zones. Your *Faces of Change 2* caring adult guide can help you explore these enablers.

ENABLER: Types	How do they enable?
Race:	
Gender:	
Geographic Location:	
Stereotypes:	
Economic:	
Religion:	
Politics:	
Appearance:	
Neighborhood:	

Talk with your *Faces of Change 2* caring adult about times in their life where they had to break out of their comfort zones. What did they do? How did they go about building comfort in another zone of interaction? Record a summary of your discussion in the space provided.

Adult Response:

4.3 CODE SWITCHING

In this unit, you will define code switching and learn how to code switch in order to expand your comfort zones. You will also learn how to recognize when moving into a zone that is dangerous.

NONCOGNITIVE VARIABLE(S)

- **REALISTIC SELF-APPRAISAL:** Recognizes and accepts any strengths and deficiencies, especially academic, and works hard at self-development. Recognizes need to broaden individuality.

- **UNDERSTANDS AND KNOWS HOW TO HANDLE THE SYSTEM:** Exhibits a realistic view of the system based upon personal experiences and is committed to improving the existing system. Takes an assertive approach to dealing with existing wrongs, but is not hostile to society nor is a "cop-out." Involves handling any "isms" (e.g., racism, sexism).

LESSON

Your work starts when you move away from the comfort of familiarity, which is doing what you like doing and doing what you know is easy. After identifying your comfort zones and understanding what they are and how they are developed, the next step is learning how to expand and move from your own zones of comfort into other zones. Remember, there are appropriate codes of conduct for every situation; the key is recognizing when the code has changed and being able to switch.

Code switching requires you to move out of your comfort zones in order to be able to operate and adapt to various situations and feel at ease wherever you are. Code switching is the ability to decipher a code of conduct in a given situation and then being able to switch or adjust your behavior to fit that situation. Code switching, because it is new, will cause a feeling of uneasiness and discomfort. The more you code switch the easier it becomes. Once you learn how to code switch, you will be doing it without much effort.

Being able to function and exist in various zones is important if you want to be able to transition into adulthood in today's society. Even if you presently live in a place where you see mainly people who look, behave, and think the way you do, that will not be the case for the rest of your life. You have to learn universal, standard codes of behavior for various zones in order to be able to move between zones. You have to learn how to code switch in order to attain success.

Have you ever taken the time to notice a little child when he/she is learning something new? They will sit and observe what is being done as if they are analyzing it in some way. Then they will begin to mimic what they have seen. Code switching is much the same in that it takes time to observe others in unfamiliar zones in order to understand it. Only at that point can you expand into that zone by code switching.

Code Switching consist of the following three steps:

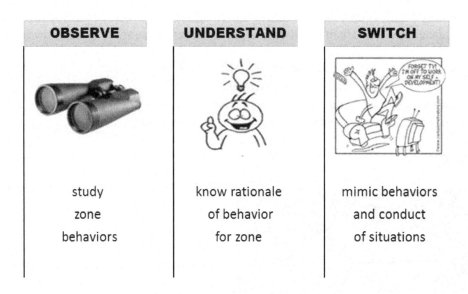

OBSERVE	UNDERSTAND	SWITCH
study zone behaviors	know rationale of behavior for zone	mimic behaviors and conduct of situations

No matter the zone, you must take time to observe the codes of behavior and understand them before you can begin to adequately explore and expand into that zone. There are, however, some codes that transcend all zones that everyone should know. We call these universal zone rules.

Observing and understanding are important in code switching, but you can't forget to practice within the new zone as well. I encourage you to take the time to do all three steps: observe (study), understand (know), and practice (mimic) so you will be prepared to expand into your new zones.

Code Switching Rules:

1. Do not overdo it
2. Recognize topics of discussion to avoid
3. Listen and learn
4. Practice and receive clarity
5. Look the part
6. Act the part
7. Learn to network

FOOD FOR THOUGHT

A Man May Change

As simply as a self-effacing bar of soap

escaping by indiscernible degrees in the wash water

is how a man may change

and still hour by hour continue in his job.

There in the mirror he appears to be on fire

but here at the office he is dust.

So long as there remains a little moisture in the stains,

he stands easily on the pavement

and moves fluidly through the corridors. If only one

cloud can be seen, it is enough to know of others,

and life stands on the brink. It rains

or it doesn't, or it rains and it rains again.

But let it go on raining for forty days and nights

or let the sun bake the ground for as long,

and it isn't life, just life, anymore, it's living.

In the meantime, in the regular weather of ordinary days,

it sometimes happens that a man has changed

so slowly that he slips away

before anyone notices

and lives and dies before anyone can find out.

Marvin Bell

WHAT YOU SHOULD KNOW

Definition of code switching

3-step process to perfect your code-switching skills

Recognize danger zones that should not be explored

ACTIVITY: 4.3.1 CODE SWITCHING

Name:	Date:

Code Switching

Having the ability to decipher a

code of behavior in a given situation

and being able to switch, or adjust,

your behavior to fit the situation.

After identifying your comfort zones, understanding what they are and how they are developed, the next step is learning how to expand and move from your own zones of comfort into other zones.

Talk About It...
Answer the following questions with your *Faces of Change 2* caring adult:

Why is it important to expand your comfort zones?

Is there anything wrong with your comfort zones now?

Think About It...
Discuss the following questions with your caring adult. Record a brief summary of your discussion in the space below.

Why is it important to learn to switch codes?

What are some code-switching situations?
1.
2.
3.
4.
5.

What are some things you might change or adjust when you code switch?
1.
2.
3.
4.
5.

In your own personal comfort zones, what are some codes of behavior?

Comfort Zone	Behavior
1.	
2.	
3.	
4.	
5.	

ACTIVITY: 4.3.2 CODE SWITCHING – PRACTICING

Name:	Date:

> "Practice isn't the thing you do once you're good. It's the thing you do that makes you good." - Malcolm Gladwell

Now What...

During the In a Zone activity, you identified some new areas you may want to stretch into and began to think about what groups of people, or behaviors you did not take the time to notice before. Now let's choose a new zone you would like to practice in order to work on your code-switching skills.

Once you've identified a new zone you would like to explore, explain why you would like to investigate it. You can choose something such as the types of food you eat or the types of people with whom you associate (*e.g. I would like to explore the world of artists because I do not have much interaction with people who are creative and into painting and other types of visual art.*)

After observing the codes for the new zone that you would like to explore, put yourself to the test and try your new zone or stretch. Answer the questions below to evaluate your exploration.

What new zone did you expand into?

MY STRETCH

_____

Area 1: Ease of switching; level of comfort

NOT EASY	1	2	3	4	5	6	7	8	9	10	VERY EASY

Area 2: Conversation

NOT EASY	1	2	3	4	5	6	7	8	9	10	VERY EASY

Area 3: Listening and learning in the midst of switching

NOT EASY	1	2	3	4	5	6	7	8	9	10	VERY EASY

Area 4: Courtesy received or given

NOT EASY	1	2	3	4	5	6	7	8	9	10	VERY EASY

Area 5: Dress

NOT EASY	1	2	3	4	5	6	7	8	9	10	VERY EASY

Area 6: Manners

NOT EASY	1	2	3	4	5	6	7	8	9	10	VERY EASY

Area 7: Connecting with others

NOT EASY	1	2	3	4	5	6	7	8	9	10	VERY EASY

How much of a stretch was it for you to expand to this new activity or zone?

NOT EASY	1	2	3	4	5	6	7	8	9	10	VERY EASY

What was the dress code for this new comfort zone?

_____ Traditional

_____ Casual (jeans or sporty wear)

_____ Business Casual (slacks, maybe a tie, usually no jacket; slacks and a blouse)

_____ Professional

_____ Formal (tuxedo; cocktail dress)

Were there clear and present zone enablers?

_____ Race

_____ Gender

_____ Education Level

_____ Culture

_____ Religion

_____ Politics

_____ Stereotypes

_____ Economic Level

_____ Appearance

_____ Where They Live

_____ Other Zone Enablers _____

Which statements best describe how you felt about the new activity/zone?

_____ I would do it again if asked.

_____ I would do it again on my own.

_____ Not interested in doing it again.

_____ This activity or zone was out of my interest area.

_____ I liked the activity/zone and will explore it more.

_____ I did not like this activity/zone but would be willing to explore others.

_____ I am willing to continue expanding into different zones.

Why?

_____

_____

5.0 REACH – WARM UP, TALENT IDENTIFICATION

You have worked hard during the *Faces of Change 2* process to be mindful of and ready for the transition that you have to make into adulthood. The idea is to help you be a successful adult. Success is really individualized. Success for one person may look one way and then be completely different for another person. You have to define success for yourself. No one can do that for you.

NONCOGNITIVE VARIABLE(S)

- **POSITIVE SELF-CONCEPT:** Demonstrates confidence, strength of character, determination, and independence.

- **REALISTIC SELF-APPRAISAL:** Recognizes and accepts any strengths and deficiencies, especially academic, and works hard at self-development. Recognizes need to broaden individuality.

LESSON

"The indispensable first step to getting

the things you want out of life is this:

decide what you want."

Ben Stein

"The biggest adventure

you can take is to live

the life of your dreams."

Oprah Winfrey

Both of the quotations above stress the importance of figuring out what you want in life, dreaming your dreams and then taking strides to make those a reality. The title of the lesson is fitting "Are we there yet?". This unit helps you to REACH forward and physically reach the destination you set for yourself. It all starts with one step. The first step you are going to perform in this unit is looking closely at your interests, skills and talents.

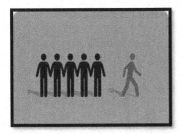

Making success a reality and transitioning into adulthood may seem completely overwhelming. At times a successful adulthood may seem to be out of reach, leaving you asking questions: Are we there yet? When do I actually become an adult? When do I know, I am truly an adult? How can I measure my progression through the maturation process? Becoming an adult is a continuous process. You must work at it daily. You are responsible for making this change in your life. Every day you grow older, every day you should move closer to successful adulthood. Some people work hard to become responsible adults; others live a lifetime exhibiting childlike behavior. Identify your talents and strive for success. Then you will reach your destination of successful adulthood.

Now is the time in your life to begin paying attention to who you are and understanding that a fun activity can turn into a passion and maybe even your lifelong career.

FOOD FOR THOUGHT

New Beginnings

It's only the beginning now
...a pathway yet unknown
At times the sound of other steps
...sometimes we walk alone

The best beginnings of our lives
May sometimes end in sorrow
But even on our darkest days
The sun will shine tomorrow.

So, we must do our very best
Whatever life may bring
And look beyond the winter chill
To smell the breath of spring.

Into each life will always come
A time to start anew
A new beginning for each heart
As fresh as morning dew.

Although the cares of life are great
And hands are bowed so low
The storms of life will leave behind
The wonder of a rainbow.

The years will never take away
Our chance to start anew
It's only the beginning now
So dreams can still come true.

Gertrude B. McClain

WHAT YOU SHOULD KNOW

Explain the importance of identifying what you want to achieve in life

Recognize your personal dreams and talent

Understand how your talents can be transformed into lifelong careers later in life

ACTIVITY: 5.0 REACH – WARM UP, TALENT IDENTIFICATION

Name:	Date:

Did you know that the interests, talents, and skills you have right now could help you figure out what it is you want to do with your life? Take a moment to complete the information below and start to explore where you want to go in life. It may be helpful to review your timelines from Unit 2.

Step 1 List the dreams, strengths, interests, talents, skills, and hobbies you currently have.	Step 2 Research and explore possible careers that may match this dream, strength, interest, talent, skill or hobby.	Step 3 Think about and list the type of schooling or training you may need in order to make this career a reality.
1.	1.	1.
2.	2.	2.
3.	3.	3.
4.	4.	4.
5.	5.	5.
6.	6.	6.
7.	7.	7.

5.1 DOLLARS AND SENSE

This unit will help you make sense of the dollars you will need to live on your own. You may have never given these issues any thought, so you will work closely together with your caring adult to figure out a cost of living for you.

NONCOGNITIVE VARIABLE(S)

- **REALISTIC SELF-APPRAISAL:** Recognizes and accepts any strengths and deficiencies, especially academic, and works hard at self-development. Recognizes need to broaden individuality.

- **UNDERSTANDS AND KNOWS HOW TO HANDLE THE SYSTEM:** Exhibits a realistic view of the system based upon personal experiences and is committed to improving the existing system. Takes an assertive approach to dealing with existing wrongs, but is not hostile to society nor is a "cop-out." Involves handling any "isms" (e.g., racism, sexism).

- **PREFERS LONG-RANGE TO SHORT-TERM OR IMMEDIATE NEEDS:** Able to respond to deferred gratification; plans ahead and sets goals.

LESSON

A large part of successful adulthood is understanding the importance of earning and budgeting money. Many look to entertainers and athletes as models for economic success. The truth is they really only account for a small percentage of financially sound individuals. Most find a career that best meets their talents and preferred lifestyle and then work hard to earn what they want and need.

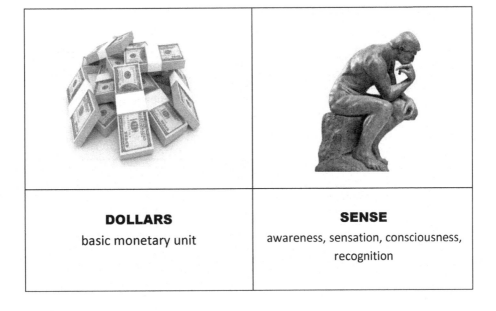

DOLLARS	SENSE
basic monetary unit	awareness, sensation, consciousness, recognition

Do you know what you need and what it costs to live? Your lifestyle should not be more extravagant than your income will allow. Hopefully you see and understand that caring for yourself financially isn't as easy as many adults make it appear.

There is one additional item that you must include in your budget: savings. You should never operate on such a tight budget that you have nothing left for savings. Your savings may start out small but you should work up to saving more and more. The goal is to have no disparity between estimated living needs and what you calculated in your sample budget.

As you grow towards adulthood, financial self-sufficiency must be a consideration for you. If there is a disparity, either your career or your lifestyle must be adjusted. Having dollars that make sense won't happen for you if you don't know how to budget and live within your means.

KEY TERMS	DEFINITIONS
Income	The general term for all the money that ends up in your hands; the amount of money generated that comes into your home or household.
Wages	A fixed regular payment, typically paid on a daily or weekly basis, made by an employer to an employee, especially to a manual or unskilled worker.
Salary	A fixed regular payment, typically paid on a monthly or biweekly basis but often expressed as an annual sum, made by an employer to an employee, especially a professional or white-collar worker.
Career	A person's chosen pursuit; a profession or occupation.
Job	A piece of work, especially a specific task, done as part of the routine of one's occupation or for an agreed price.
Cost of Living	The average cost of the basic necessities of life, such as food, shelter, and clothing.
Necessity	Something essential, required, or indispensable food, shelter, etc.
Luxury	A pleasure out of the ordinary allowed to oneself.
Bills	An amount of money owed for goods supplied or services rendered, set out in a printed or written statement of charges.
Benefits	A payment or gift made by an employer. (e.g. pension plan, free health insurance, and other benefits).

Let's see what income you think it will take for you to live the life you want. You have to consider all that is a part of living and taking care of yourself, such as what kind of housing you will have, what type of vehicle you will drive, how much money you will spend each day, how much you need for food, etc. You also must keep in mind a realistic amount of income for the career you will have. If you plan to work at a retail store as a salesperson, you probably won't make $60,000 per year. Your lifestyle must match your income. If not, financial instability will follow when you live outside your income.

Now you have to take step two to see if the amount that you chose really makes sense by looking at a detailed budget of how the money you make will be spent. Right now, you probably do not own a home or have a job that will support you without assistance. For the most part, your parents/guardians bear the responsibility of your care. Imagine if today you were informed that from this moment forward you would have to take care of yourself.

Your dollars must make sense. Since you may have never given this issue any thought, you may want to work closely with your caring adult or maybe even go online to determine the average cost for each line item in this exercise. Based on personal experience, your caring adult can assist in being realistic with your dollars and sense.

FOOD FOR THOUGHT

Forbes Top Ten Money Quotes

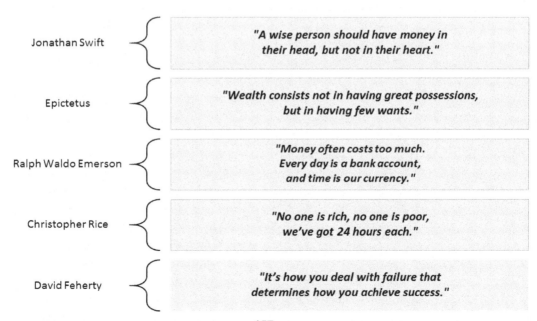

Jonathan Swift — *"A wise person should have money in their head, but not in their heart."*

Epictetus — *"Wealth consists not in having great possessions, but in having few wants."*

Ralph Waldo Emerson — *"Money often costs too much. Every day is a bank account, and time is our currency."*

Christopher Rice — *"No one is rich, no one is poor, we've got 24 hours each."*

David Feherty — *"It's how you deal with failure that determines how you achieve success."*

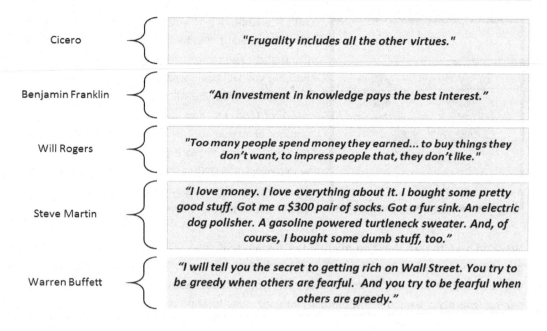

Cicero — *"Frugality includes all the other virtues."*

Benjamin Franklin — *"An investment in knowledge pays the best interest."*

Will Rogers — *"Too many people spend money they earned... to buy things they don't want, to impress people that, they don't like."*

Steve Martin — *"I love money. I love everything about it. I bought some pretty good stuff. Got me a $300 pair of socks. Got a fur sink. An electric dog polisher. A gasoline powered turtleneck sweater. And, of course, I bought some dumb stuff, too."*

Warren Buffett — *"I will tell you the secret to getting rich on Wall Street. You try to be greedy when others are fearful. And you try to be fearful when others are greedy."*

WHAT YOU SHOULD KNOW

The importance of finances in being a successful adult

Estimate the amount it will take to live the life you want to live

Identify aspects of a budget that must be considered in determining the income needed for your preferred lifestyle

ACTIVITY: 5.1 DOLLARS AND SENSE

Name:		Date:

To the best of your ability complete the following activity. Be sure to make all necessary calculations before sharing with your caring adult. Complete answers based on monthly payments to calculate the estimated income you will need to support your projected lifestyle.

Review your answers with your caring adult. Find out whether the adult agrees or disagrees with your answers and why. After you have reviewed your answers with an adult, make necessary changes.

Note: As you calculate, remember that some bills are necessary while others are a luxury. The more luxuries, the higher your cost of living.

> **What amount of money do you think you would need in order to live for a year?**
>
> $ _____

Calculate your estimated yearly income into an hourly wage.

> Yearly $ _____ / 52 weeks
>
> = $ _____ Weekly

> Weekly $ _____ / 40 hours
>
> = $ _____ Hourly

Calculate your estimated cost of living.

HOUSING – check one	**ENTERTAINMENT**
$ _____ House (mortgage/rent) $ _____ Apartment (rent) $ _____ Condo/Townhouse (mortgage/rent) $ _____ Loft (mortgage/rent) MONTHLY COST $ _____	$_____ Movies $_____ Eating out $_____ Recreational Activities $_____ Concerts $_____ Other_____ $_____ Other_____ MONTHLY COST $ _____
TRANSPORTATION – check one	**OTHER LIVING EXPENSES** – cost per
$ _____ Car Note $ _____ Car insurance $ _____ Car maintenance $ _____ Car Gasoline $ _____ Public transportation $ _____ Taxi/Uber/Other MONTHLY COST $ _____	$ _____ Healthcare $ _____ Toiletries $ _____ Clothing (including shoes and undergarments) $ _____ other $ _____ other MONTHLY COST $ _____
BILLS – cost per	**SAVINGS**
$ _____ Electric $ _____ Water $ _____ Cable $ _____ Phone $ _____ Internet $ _____ Gas $ _____ Waste Management $ _____ Cell Phone $ _____ Furniture $ _____ Groceries $ _____ Home maintenance $ _____ other $ _____ other MONTHLY COST $ _____	MONTHLY SAVING $ _____
COMBINED MONTHLY COST	**TOTAL MONTHLY COST OF LIVING**
$ _____ Housing $ _____ Transportation $ _____ Utilities $ _____ Living $ _____ Entertainment $ _____ Savings	$ _____

Calculate your estimated yearly income needed.

Note: Add, as a minimum, an additional 25% to your income that you must pay to the government for taxes before you get paid.

TOTAL MONTHLY COST OF LIVING	ACTUAL YEARLY INCOME NEEDED
$ _____ X 12 =	$ _____

Compare the actual income figure you calculated above to the estimated figure you listed at the beginning of this exercise.

Is the estimated figure more or less than the calculated amount?

How big of a difference are the two figures?

All the money in the world will not matter if it does not make sense.

Have you ever stopped to think about how much money you will need to live?

Do you know how much money you need to make to live an average decent life?

What is your estimated cost for living on your own?

What bills will you have to pay each month?

How much money will you need to pay your bills?

Which bills are necessary and which bills are luxuries?

5.2 SUCCESS IS . . .

You have spent a large part of your time in this course working on being a successful adult. But just what is success? Have you ever defined success for yourself? Do you look around at others for your definition? In this unit, you will realize what it takes to be a success.

NONCOGNITIVE VARIABLE(S)

- **POSITIVE SELF-CONCEPT:** Demonstrates confidence, strength of character, determination, and independence.

- **REALISTIC SELF-APPRAISAL:** Recognizes and accepts any strengths and deficiencies, especially academic, and works hard at self-development. Recognizes need to broaden individuality.

- **PREFERS LONG-RANGE TO SHORT-TERM OR IMMEDIATE NEEDS:** Able to respond to deferred gratification; plans ahead and sets goals.

LESSON

Everyone can be successful. You need only to have the traits that will allow you to obtain your specific definition of success. There are four pillars of success that everyone must possess. Whatever your definition of success, these pillars will form the framework for that definition.

4 KEY PILLARS OF SUCCESS	
1. SELF-SUFFICIENCY the ability to provide for yourself	**2. EMPLOYABILITY** the skills and training needed to help you obtain employment
3. FINANCIAL STABILITY the ability to make sound economic decisions and maintain financial success	**4. ETHICAL CODE/LIVE BY** always do unto others what you would like done to you (*the golden rule*)

It is important to surround yourself with others who also are seeking success. It helps to keep you on track. Having models for success is equally as important. Take a look back at the list of people you identified as being successful in an earlier unit.

Regardless of the level of success you attempt to achieve, it all starts with a plan. You must develop your ideas on who and what constitute success for you as you create your own definition of success.

FOOD FOR THOUGHT

You Can If You Think You Can

If you think you are beaten, you are;
If you think you dare not, you don't!
If you'd like to win, but you think you can't,
It's almost certain you won't.

If you think you'll lose, you're lost;
For out in the world we find
Success begins with a fellow's will;
It's all in the state of mind!

If you think you're outclassed, you are;
You've got to think high to rise.
You've got to be sure of yourself
Before you'll ever win the prize.

Life's battles don't always go
To the stronger or faster man;
But sooner or later the man who wins
Is the person who thinks he can!

Walter D. Wintle

WHAT YOU SHOULD KNOW

Identify the four pillars of success

Define what success means to you

Recognize the traits of success in others

ACTIVITY: 5.2 SUCCESS IS . . .

Name:	Date:

List examples for each of the 4 KEY PILLARS OF SUCCESS that show them in action.

SELF-SUFFICIENCY – the ability to provide for yourself (example: earning money through gainful employment)

1.

2.

3.

EMPLOYABILITY – the skills and training needed to help you obtain employment

1.

2.

3.

FINANCIAL STABILITY – the ability to make sound economic decisions and maintain financial success

1.

2.

3.

ETHICAL CODE/LIVE BY – always do unto others what you would like done to you (*the golden rule*)

1.

2.

3.

While ideas of success may differ, these four pillars remain the same. They are the traits that should and will typify a person who would be called successful. Do all the people you listed in the earlier unit possess these four traits?

Do your models for success exhibit one or all of the KEY PILLARS OF SUCCESS?

How do you see these traits exhibited in their lives? For each person listed in the column on the left, circle each pillar they possess.

PEOPLE	KEY PILLARS OF SUCCESS			
Parents	SELF-SUFFICIENCY	EMPLOYABILITY	FINANCIAL STABILITY	ETHICAL CODE/ LIVE BY
Teachers	SELF-SUFFICIENCY	EMPLOYABILITY	FINANCIAL STABILITY	ETHICAL CODE/ LIVE BY
Grandparents	SELF-SUFFICIENCY	EMPLOYABILITY	FINANCIAL STABILITY	ETHICAL CODE/ LIVE BY
Mentors	SELF-SUFFICIENCY	EMPLOYABILITY	FINANCIAL STABILITY	ETHICAL CODE/ LIVE BY
Role Models	SELF-SUFFICIENCY	EMPLOYABILITY	FINANCIAL STABILITY	ETHICAL CODE/ LIVE BY
Family Member	SELF-SUFFICIENCY	EMPLOYABILITY	FINANCIAL STABILITY	ETHICAL CODE/ LIVE BY
Neighbors	SELF-SUFFICIENCY	EMPLOYABILITY	FINANCIAL STABILITY	ETHICAL CODE/ LIVE BY
Others	SELF-SUFFICIENCY	EMPLOYABILITY	FINANCIAL STABILITY	ETHICAL CODE/ LIVE BY
Others	SELF-SUFFICIENCY	EMPLOYABILITY	FINANCIAL STABILITY	ETHICAL CODE/ LIVE BY

5.3 ROAD MAP TO SUCCESS

In this unit, you will be introduced to the road map to success which will allow you to understand that achieving success is a journey.

NONCOGNITIVE VARIABLE(S)

- **POSITIVE SELF-CONCEPT:** Demonstrates confidence, strength of character, determination, and independence.

- **REALISTIC SELF-APPRAISAL:** Recognizes and accepts any strengths and deficiencies, especially academic, and works hard at self-development. Recognizes need to broaden individuality.

- **PREFERS LONG-RANGE TO SHORT-TERM OR IMMEDIATE NEEDS:** Able to respond to deferred gratification; plans ahead and sets goals.

LESSON

When you hear the phrase Road Trip, you probably picture a group of family and/or friends in a car heading off to some fun destination. You make preparations and plans for the trip, where you will stop to rest, eat, what sights you may take time to see. Before the days of GPS and Google Maps, the way you planned for a road trip was viewing a map to determine the route you would take to reach your destination.

Planning your trip to success is very much the same as the planning you would do for any road trip. When planning a physical road trip, there are five components that must be considered. Each component you use in planning a road trip corresponds directly to planning your success. By using these same components, you can chart a roadmap to your success.

Your goals and dreams will dictate how you plan for success. As a part of your plan you will have to determine the time needed to achieve success and the education needed to prepare. It's important to plan well because on your journey to success you will spend a lot of time at your final destination - you will be there a lifetime.

ROAD TRIP COMPONENTS

- **Destination** - the place to which someone or something is going or being sent.
- **Route** - a way or course taken in getting from a starting point to a destination.
- **Distance** - an amount of space between two things or people.
- **Preparation** - action or process of being ready for use or consideration.
- **Length of stay** - a term to describe the duration of a single episode.

SUCCESS COMPONENTS

- **Destination** - Goals, dreams, success
- **Route** - Your plan
- **Distance** - Time needed to get to your destination
- **Preparation** - Type of education/training
- **Length of stay** – Lifetime

FOOD FOR THOUGHT

Uphill

Does the road wind up-hill all the way?

Yes, to the very end.

Will the day's journey take the whole long day?

From morn to night, my friend.

But is there for the night a resting-place?

A roof for when the slow dark hours begin.

May not the darkness hide it from my face?

You cannot miss that inn.

Shall I meet other wayfarers at night?

Those who have gone before.

Then must I knock, or call when just in sight?

They will not keep you standing at that door.

Shall I find comfort, travel-sore and weak?

Of labor you shall find the sum.

Will there be beds for me and all who seek?

Yea, beds for all who come.

Christina Rossetti

WHAT YOU SHOULD KNOW

Understand that achieving success is a journey

Five components needed for your journey to success

Recognize that the journey to success requires planning

ACTIVITY: 5.3 ROAD MAP TO SUCCESS

Name:	Date:

Having a destination and a plan that takes into account all the necessary preparation needed can make a world of difference in where you spend your lifetime. Planning your trip to success is very much the same as planning a road trip. Complete your plans for each one of the success components and take a good look at the road you are traveling.

SUCCESS COMPONENTS

DESTINATION

Where are you going?

ROUTE

How will you get there?

DISTANCE

How long will it take you to get there?

PREPARATION

What do you need to do to be prepared for the trip?

LENGTH

How long are you going to be at your destination?

5.4 HAVE, DO, BE – CREATING GOAL STATEMENTS

In this unit, you will create your personal goal statements and make an action plan for realizing your goals.

NONCOGNITIVE VARIABLE(S)

- **REALISTIC SELF-APPRAISAL:** Recognizes and accepts any strengths and deficiencies, especially academic, and works hard at self-development. Recognizes need to broaden individuality.

- **PREFERS LONG-RANGE TO SHORT-TERM OR IMMEDIATE NEEDS:** Able to respond to deferred gratification; plans ahead and sets goals.

- **POSITIVE SELF-CONCEPT:** Demonstrates confidence, strength of character, determination, and independence.

LESSON

Most sporting events are based on scoring points. Usually, as in basketball, hockey, soccer and football, the closer you are to the goal the better chance you will have to score. Your goals in life are a lot like the games just mentioned. Being close to your personal goals increases your odds of obtaining them. Your goals are simply anything you would like to have, do, or be.

People don't plan to fail they fail to plan. Having a plan is half of the battle of being successful. The other half of the battle is working towards achieving your goals. You may change or adjust some of your goals with growth and maturing. You may have to adjust your action plan as well. Adjustments are to be expected, but halting progress should not be an option. You can reach your goals; you need only to plan to succeed.

Having goals is wonderful, but you have to have a plan of action to achieve goals or they will never come to fruition. There are steps you will have to take now to achieve your goals and steps later as well.

For the purpose of this unit you can define a goal as anything you would like to HAVE, DO, or BE!

HAVE	DO	BE
What are the things in life you want to own?	What are those things in life you want to accomplish?	What is it that you want to ensue?

FOOD FOR THOUGHT

A Goal in Life

What do you do
when you've pursued a dream
and finally
made it come true,
do you find another dream
and start pursuing it to?
The answer is simple, yes
that is what you have to do.
Just keep pursuing all your dreams
no matter how wild
they may seem.
You have to have
a goal in life
and our dreams are that goal.
We have to pursue them,

each and every one
to the bitter end,
for if we don't we will end up
with a wasted life.
I thought once
I'd given up mine,
but that was just a rest bite.
I came back
refreshed, renewed
and pursued my dream
even harder than before
until finally
I made it happen
and made one of my dreams
come true.

David Harris

WHAT YOU SHOULD KNOW

Identify your goals on the Have, Do, Be chart

Recognize what can be done now and later in order to realize your goals

Understand the need to identify goals and plan for achieving them

ACTIVITY: 5.4 HAVE, DO, BE – CREATING GOAL STATEMENTS

Name:	Date:

Setting Goals

HAVE – DO – BE

Having goals is essential in life. If you don't have a destination, you will never get anywhere. Creating your goals is a two-step process:

STEP 1: Complete HAVE, DO, BE chart. Take some time to think about all that you would like to have, do and be. Record your thoughts on the chart below to help you identify your goals. Share these goals with your caring adult.

I would like to **HAVE** (example: a college degree, house, car etc.)

1.

2.

3.

4.

5.

I would Like to **DO** (example: I would like to travel the world)

1.

2.

3.

4.

5.

I would like to **BE** (example: a doctor)

1.

2.

3.

4.

5.

Step 2: Create Your Goal Statements to help you obtain the things on your **HAVE – DO – BE** list.

Now that you have identified what you would like to have, do, and be, it is now time to create your goal statements that will help you take action towards achieving that goal. Your caring adult's assistance and guidance will be helpful during this activity they can help to keep these goals in the forefront daily.

A. Prioritize Goals – Using the chart on the previous page, list the goals you want to achieve in order of importance.

GOAL 1:	GOAL 2:	GOAL 3:

B. Action Plan – Below in the column labeled **HAVE – DO – BE,** list your goals in the order of importance as you indicated above. In the column, next to that goal labeled **NOW,** list those things you can do now to achieve that one particular goal. In the next column labeled **LATER,** list those things you can do later to achieve that same particular goal (when applicable give a time frame).

HAVE-DO-BE	NOW	LATER
<u>Example</u> Graduate from college	<u>Example</u> 1. Stay in school 2. Choose area of interest 3. Earn good grades	<u>Example</u> 1. Apply to college 2. Choose area of study 3. Take college entrance exam
GOAL 1	<u>Goal 1</u> 1. 2. 3.	<u>Goal 1</u> 1. 2. 3.
GOAL 2	<u>Goal 2</u> 1. 2. 3.	<u>Goal 2</u> 1. 2. 3.

GOAL 3	Goal 3	Goal 3
	1.	1.
	2.	2.
	3.	3.
GOAL 4	Goal 4	Goal 4
	1.	1.
	2.	2.
	3.	3.
GOAL 5	Goal 5	Goal 5
	1.	1.
	2.	2.
	3.	3.
GOAL 6	Goal 6	Goal 6
	1.	1.
	2.	2.
	3.	3.
GOAL 7	Goal 7	Goal 7
	1.	1.
	2.	2.
	3.	3.
GOAL 8	Goal 8	Goal 8
	1.	1.
	2.	2.
	3.	3.

5.5 TEN MOST POWERFUL TWO LETTER WORDS IN THE WORLD!

In this unit, you will be introduced to the "10 Most Powerful 2 - Letter Words". They will also create your own "If It Is To Be, It Is Up To Me" statements to reaffirm your personal power and responsibility for your success.

NONCOGNITIVE VARIABLE(S)

- **POSITIVE SELF-CONCEPT:** Demonstrates confidence, strength of character, determination, and independence.

- **REALISTIC SELF-APPRAISAL:** Recognizes and accepts any strengths and deficiencies, especially academic, and works hard at self-development. Recognizes need to broaden individuality.

- **PREFERS LONG-RANGE TO SHORT-TERM OR IMMEDIATE NEEDS:** Able to respond to deferred gratification; plans ahead and sets goals.

LESSON

two letter words			
of	if	up	by
no	it	me	do
be	an	to	my
go	us	is	at

You have the power within to achieve the goals you have set and reach the heights you dream of reaching. You have worked through activities in *Faces of Change 2* that have equipped you with some important skills needed for the journey to productive adulthood. It is up to you to decide what you want and then do what needs to be done to get results.

Emily Dickinson wrote … "A word is dead when it is said, some say, I say it just begins to live that day." Emily Dickenson's poem reminds us just how powerful words are. They can be permanent influences on us in many ways. There are ten simple, two-letter words that, when strung together, become the ten most important, powerful words in the world in regard to your life and your transition to successful adulthood.

IF IT IS TO BE, IT IS UP TO ME

It matters not how strait the gate,

How charged with punishments the scroll,

I am the master of my fate:

I am the captain of my soul.

William Ernest Henley

This Henley excerpt from the poem Invictus is a great one to commit to memory. It is a reminder that no matter what, you have the ability and the responsibility to create your own success. Never forget that you have the power within to do whatever it is you want to do in your life. If it is to be, it is up to you.

FOOD FOR THOUGHT

A Word

A WORD is dead

When it is said,

Some say.

I say it just

Begins to live

That day.

Emily Dickinson

WHAT YOU SHOULD KNOW

The 10 most powerful two letter words

Understand how powerful words are

Recognize your own power to determine your personal success

ACTIVITY: 5.5 TEN MOST POWERFUL TWO LETTER WORDS IN THE WORLD!

Name:	Date:

You have the power within to achieve the goals you have set and attain the heights you dream of reaching. You have worked through activities in *Faces of Change 2* to equip you with some important skills needed for the journey to successful and productive adulthood. It is up to you to decide what you want and what you need to do to get it. Using the information from all of the previous units, insert a word or phrase to complete the IF IT IS TO BE statements below.

IF _____GOING TO COLLEGE_____(IT) IS TO BE, IT IS UP TO ME!

IF _____(IT) IS TO BE, IT IS UP TO ME!

IF _____(IT) IS TO BE, IT IS UP TO ME!

IF _____(IT) IS TO BE, IT IS UP TO ME!

IF _____(IT) IS TO BE, IT IS UP TO ME!

I am the master of my fate: I am the captain of my soul.

William Ernest Henley

Reflect...

William Henley's poem "Invictus" ends with this statement: "I am the master of my fate; I am the captain of my soul." Taking into consideration the ten most powerful two-letter words in the world, how are you the master of your fate and the captain of your soul? What does this statement mean to you?

FACES OF CHANGE LIVE BY

I did not have any control over my birth.
I also do not have any control of change, it is inevitable.
As I travel my life's journey I will continue to be confronted with change.
I will be ready and equipped for change.
Armed with the necessary skills needed to face the change.

I have discovered the reason why I was born.
I will reach beyond my current situation.
I will dream big dreams, and aspire to do great things.
Always striving to be my very best.
I have all that I need within me, to do have, do or be whatever want.
I can do everything that I think I can.

I will learn from the knowledge, wisdom, courage, and experiences
of the elders and those that came before me.
I do not have to experience a mistake to learn from it.
If someone else has already learned that lesson, I can learn from their experiences.

I must remember those heroes in my life and go to them
for advice during times of confusion and misunderstanding.
Faces of Change does not stop at the end of this book.
This process is fluent therefore, I must revisit my timeline and update my plans and goals.

As I move from one phase of life to the next,
I will build and master those skills in my present phase of life.
Thus, being better prepared to move forward to the next phase.

I will deliberately grow my comfort zones often.
I will grow my world;
I will not stand still waiting on life to come to me.
I must go get it.

Life will not just happen to me.
I will design and orchestrate the way I live my life.
I am the master, pilot, navigator, and captain of my fate.

Consciously controlling my surroundings
I will only be found in positive productive environments.
Becoming a product of the environments I spend my time in.
Choosing my friends as if I were choosing the most important thing I ever had to choose in life.

I am committed to myself and no one else.
My time will not be wasted trying to control others;
I will use that time improving myself.
Never sitting idle doing nothing, always working to improve myself9.

I will never ever allow myself to have a bad day, maybe a bad moment.
I must immediately recover from that bad moment;
Bad days turn into weeks, weeks to months, months to a year.
I will control what I think.
What I think about I bring about.

I will not make excuses;
If I do, excuses can consume me.

I trust and believe in the power of good sound relationships;
I do not discard the power of a relationship.
I will not be afraid to develop healthy relationships with adults I admire, love, and respect.
The right relationship with the right person can be the determining factor in whether I succeed or fail.
Adults and youth must work together As I assume the responsibilities of being an adult.

As I successfully go through the different phases of life,
I will sacrifice to be a hero to young people coming along after me.
I will share my life experiences with those younger than I.
I will not allow a Great Divide to grow between me and the next generation.
I will work with them as my caring adult has guided and worked with me.
Assisting them with developing skills to face their change.

Made in the USA
Columbia, SC
05 February 2018